WILLIAM WORDSWORTH
SELECTED POEMS

William Wordsworth by Henry Edridge, 1806.

WILLIAM WORDSWORTH

Selected Poems

Edited by Stephen Hebron

THE WORDSWORTH TRUST

GRASMERE

Published by the Wordsworth Trust,
Dove Cottage, Grasmere, Cumbria

©2008 All rights reserved

ISBN 978 1 905256 36 5

Designed by Stephen Hebron

Set in 11/14 pt Monotype Bulmer
Printed by Titus Wilson, Kendal

CONTENTS

LATER POEMS:

An evening view of Ullswater by Joseph Wright of Derby, 1789.
The landscape of Wordsworth's childhood.

WILLIAM WORDSWORTH

A Biography

William Wordsworth was born on 7 April 1770 in Cockermouth, a small market town in the north-west corner of the English Lake District. He was the second son of John Wordsworth, a lawyer, and Ann Cookson. An elder brother, Richard, had been born two years earlier. His only sister, Dorothy, was born in 1771, and two younger brothers, John and Christopher, were born in 1772 and 1774 respectively.

Wordsworth always considered himself fortunate in his birthplace, for as a child in Cockermouth he grew up around nature. His earliest memory was the gentle voice of the Derwent, 'the fairest of all rivers', that ran along the bottom of the garden, and which 'loved / To blend his murmurs with my nurse's song'. Later, as a five year-old, he would go swimming in the river, and make 'one long bathing of a summer's day'; at other times he would run 'Over the sandy fields, leaping through groves / Of yellow grunsel', or, 'alone / Beneath the sky', would 'run abroad in wantonness, to sport, / A naked Savage, in the thunder shower'.

In 1778 Wordsworth's mother went to London to visit a friend. There she became ill, apparently after sleeping in a damp bed, and less than two months later she was dead. 'Early died / My honoured mother', Wordsworth wrote many years later, 'she who was the heart / And hinge of all our learnings and our love'. With her death, the existence that he knew and loved at Cockermouth came to an end. Dorothy, his constant friend and companion, was sent to live with cousins in Halifax, a hundred miles away in Yorkshire. They were not to see each other again for nine years. Then, in May 1779, he and his brother Richard were sent to the grammar school at Hawkshead, a village thirty miles to the south, in the heart of the Lake District.

Hawkshead lies at the head of Esthwaite Water, one of the region's smaller lakes. In Wordsworth's day it was a secluded spot, and its inhabitants formed a close, industrious community. They were farmers, labourers and shepherds, builders and joiners, blacksmiths, bakers and shopkeepers. The unassuming dignity of these 'plain living people' – 'the quiet woodman in the woods, / The shepherd on the hills' – made a deep impression on the young Wordsworth. The grammar school had been founded in 1585 and had a fine reputation. The curriculum concentrated on those subjects essential for future academic success – Latin and Greek, mathematics and science – but Wordsworth was also encouraged to read literature. At Cockermouth his father had urged him to learn 'large portions of Shakespeare and Milton' by heart. Now, at Hawkshead, he built upon this foundation. Wordsworth read all he could; he was, the headmaster's son recollected, 'one of the very few boys, who used to read the old books in the school library'. He was also encouraged to write, and it was at this time, Wordsworth later said, that he first became 'open to the charm / Of words in tuneful order, found them sweet / For *their own sakes*—a passion and a power'.

At the end of 1783 Wordsworth's father died. Now an orphan, Wordsworth remained at Hawkshead Grammar School for a further two and a half years. His final year there, 1787, was a memorable one. In March he became a published poet, when his sonnet, 'On hearing Miss Helen Maria Williams weep at a Tale of Distress', appeared in the *European Magazine* under the pseudonym 'Axiologus'. He also embarked upon his first long poem, 'The Vale of Esthwaite', of which only fragments now survive. Then, in June, 'after separation desolate', he was at last reunited with Dorothy at Penrith. Together with a childhood friend, Mary Hutchinson, they explored the countryside around the River Eamont, spending many hours among the ruins of Brougham Castle, where they would lie on the ground, 'listening to the wild-flowers and the grass / As they gave out their whispers to the wind'. But the reunion was all too brief. At the end of October brother and sister were again separated, when Wordsworth left Penrith for the south, and St. John's College, Cambridge University.

Cambridge and the Alps, 1787–91

During his first weeks at Cambridge Wordsworth's spirits were high. The unfamiliar sights and sounds of the ancient city enthralled him. He also began well academically, scoring highly in his initial examinations. But the strong sense of rootedness he had known at Cockermouth and Hawkshead was not to be repeated at Cambridge. Before long, his sense of purpose started to weaken, and, once 'the first glitter of the show was passed', his mind rebounded 'into its former self'. His uncle, William Cookson, confidently expected him to sit for an honours degree and become a senior member of St. John's College, or failing that, a lawyer like his father. Neither prospect appealed to Wordsworth. His overriding feeling was he was 'not for that hour / Nor for that place'; he was 'ill-tutored for captivity', and wanted to pursue a course of study that had 'an ampler range / And freer pace'. So, 'detached / Internally from academic cares', he explored the Cambridgeshire countryside, and read widely. He engaged a private tutor to teach him Italian, made his own translations of Virgil, and deepened his already considerable knowledge of the English poets.

Significantly, for his first two summer vacations, in 1788 and 1789, Wordsworth left Cambridge and headed straight for Hawkshead. This was still his real home, and he found himself greeting old friends 'doubtless with a little pride / But more with shame, for my habiliments, / The transformation, and the gay attire'. He was also writing: not, to his uncle's chagrin, verses he had been invited to compose to commemorate the death of the Master of St. John's that year, but a long poem, *An Evening Walk*, addressed to Dorothy and celebrating the beauties of his native landscape.

For his final summer vacation, however, Wordsworth was altogether more ambitious. On 13 July 1790 he and a Cambridge friend from North Wales, Thomas Jones, set sail from Dover, bound for France. They landed at Calais that evening, and the next morning began a twelve-week walking tour of the Continent. It was an intoxicating time to travel through France, for the country was, as Wordsworth put it in a letter to Dorothy, 'mad with joy in consequence of the revolution'. In May the previous year, King Louis XVI, in an attempt to maintain control over his debt-ridden country, had summoned his parliament, the States-General, but by July had been forced to replace the States-General with a National Assembly, and absolute political power had passed out of the hands of the aristocracy. On 14 July, the Bastille, the Paris fortress which symbolised the old feudal order, had been stormed and destroyed. Wordsworth and Jones were starting their walking tour on the very anniversary of this momentous event, which had come to mark the beginning of the French Revolution. As they left Calais, the Fête de la Fédération was being celebrated in Paris, and the King was swearing an oath of allegiance to the new constitution.

In time, Wordsworth was to follow the course of the Revolution closely and embrace its ideals, but what interested him now was not politics but scenery, specifically, the sublime landscape of the Alps, which he and Jones now proceeded to explore with remarkable energy. From Calais they travelled, on foot and by boat, some five hundred miles south to Lyons. Then they turned east and walked to the mountains around the monastery of the Grande Chartreuse, described by the poet Thomas Gray in 1719 as 'one of the most poetical scenes imaginable'. Here, for the only time on the entire trip, they allowed themselves a day's rest. From the Chartreuse they walked north to Lake Geneva, and then on to the great glaciers of Chamonix, and the Alps' highest peak, Mont Blanc. They crossed the Alps over the Simplon Pass, and descend-

'The Lower Part of the Valley and Glacier of Chamouny',
engraved by William Woollett after William Pars, 1773.

ed into Italy through the Ravine of Gondo. From here they
proceeded to the lakes at Maggiore, Lugano and Como, and
then on to Lake Lucerne and Lake Zurich. From Zurich they
travelled along the Rhine to the falls at Schaffhausen. At Basel
they bought a boat and navigated down the Rhine to Cologne.
They returned to England, via Ostend, around 11 October. It
had been a magnificent achievement. In a little less than three
months, Wordsworth and Jones had covered, mostly on foot,
almost three thousand miles.

Wordsworth returned for his final term at Cambridge, and
in January 1791 graduated with only a pass, rather than a full
honours degree. He had little idea what he would do now, and
idled his way through the next few months while his guard-
ians, on whom he was still financially dependent, tried, unsuc-
cessfully, to persuade him into various careers. 'I am doomed
to be an idler thro[ughout] my whole life', he confessed to a
Cambridge friend, William Matthews, in November. But he
had, at least, a plan for the winter: he would go to Orléans, a
town just south of Paris, and learn French.

A view of Paris by David Cox, 1829.

France and London: 1791–5

Wordsworth left England on 26 November, and four days later reached Paris. He spent the next five days sightseeing, seeking out places that had been made famous by the Revolution: Montmartre, a favourite meeting place for revolutionaries; the Field of Mars, where the Fête de la Fédération had been held on 14 July 1790; the Pantheon, now the burial place of Voltaire and Rousseau; the National Assembly, and the Jacobin Club.

From Paris Wordsworth took the fifty-mile journey south to Orléans, where he stayed until early February 1792. He then moved on to Blois, a town lying twenty miles to the south east. Here he met Michel Beaupuy, a French army captain. Though of noble birth, and a member of a largely Royalist regiment, Beaupuy was a dedicated revolutionary. In the few weeks of their friendship, he was to give Wordsworth some idea of the complicated political events which were then transforming France. Far more importantly, he was a living embodiment of revolutionary principles; he was a man, Wordsworth later wrote, who 'through the events / Of that great change wandered in perfect faith'. Thanks to Beaupuy, Wordsworth ceased to look upon the Revolution with the detached curiosity of a tourist, and became fully committed to its ideals. In his own words, he became 'a patriot – and my heart was all / Given to the people, and my love was theirs'.

But this was not all. During these intense, vivid months in France, Wordsworth also became a father. In Orléans he had become intimate with a local girl, Annette Vallon. By September, it was clear that Annette was carrying their child, and the following month Wordsworth left for England, seemingly with the intention of raising enough money to enable him to return and marry Annette. By the time his and Annette's daughter, Caroline, was baptized at Orléans Cathedral on 15 December, he was back in London. Then political events took over, and he found himself unable to return to France: on 1 February 1793, France declared war on England, and safe travel between the two countries became impossible. Wordsworth was not to see Annette and Caroline for another ten years. Such are the basic facts, but of the emotions and circumstances behind them we know very little. Wordsworth never refered to Annette directly in his poetry, and neither he or his family ever talked about her at length in their letters or journals.

After his formative experiences in France, Wordsworth now struggled to come to terms with life back in England. The next three years were to be among the most difficult of his life. He had no income, and few intentions. His new-found republicanism made him an outsider, 'one of that odious class of men called democrats'. In France, he had a daughter who he had never seen. One of the first things he did was to publish, in January 1793, his two most substantial works to date, *An Evening Walk* and *Descriptive Sketches*. The latter celebrated his 1790 tour of the Alps with Robert Jones, and had mostly been written in Orléans the previous summer. He had little confidence in either of them as poems, but, he told Matthews the following year, 'as I had done nothing by which to distinguish myself at the university, I thought these little things might shew that I could do something'. His next work, a political tract entitled *A Letter to the Bishop of Llandaff*, showed him at his most fiercely republican. He argued for universal suffrage, and with it the abolition of both monarchy and aristocracy. Violence, even the execution of a king, he maintained, was justifiable in the early stages of a revolution. It was probably fortunate for Wordsworth that he never, in the end, published this; had he done so, he may well have found himself on trial for treason.

In July Wordsworth spent a month on the Isle of Wight with an old schoolfriend, William Calvert. Every day he would watch, with bitter feelings, the English fleet off Portsmouth preparing itself for the war with France. On the return journey north he parted with Calvert at Salisbury, and spent several days wandering alone over Salisbury Plain. He came upon the prehistoric remains of Stonehenge, and there, introverted and depressed, and 'by the solitude o'ercome', he imagined the savagery of ancient Britain: in his mind the place became a 'sacrificial altar, fed / with living men', and he saw, 'here and there, / A single Briton in his wolf-skin vest / With shield and stone-axe, stride across the Wold'. Shortly afterwards he began 'Salisbury Plain', a bleak poem in which two outcasts, a solitary traveller and a homeless woman, speak of their misfortunes while taking shelter from a storm. From Salisbury Plain Wordsworth headed north, via Bath, Bristol and the Wye Valley, to Robert Jones's home in Wales, where he seems to have stayed for a little over a month. For the rest of that year, his movements are uncertain.

'I have been doing nothing, and still continue to be doing nothing', Wordsworth wrote despondently to Matthews in February the following year, 'What is to become of me I know not'. But that month he was reunited with Dorothy in Halifax, and her company had its usual stabilising influence. In April they went to stay with William Calvert at his home, Windy Brow, near Keswick in the northern part of the Lake District.

There Wordsworth revised 'Salisbury Plain' and *An Evening Walk*, and looked after William Calvert's younger brother Raisley, who was dangerously ill with tuberculosis. That autumn, Wordsworth offered to accompany Raisley to Lisbon, thinking that the warm climate would improve Raisley's health. In October they set off, but within hours Raisely's worsening condition forced them to turn back. Twelve weeks later, in January 1795, Raisley died, but not before he had made a remarkable gift: in his will, he had bequeathed Wordsworth the sum of £900. The purpose of this, Wordsworth explained to his brother Richard, was 'to set me above want and to enable me to pursue my literary views or any other views with greater success'. Raisley's bequest, in itself an extraordinary vote of confidence, offered the chance of a life of independence and creative achievement. 'He cleared a passage for me', Wordsworth later wrote, 'and the stream / Flowed in the bent of Nature'.

By the end of January Wordsworth was back was in London, and there forged a number of long-lasting friendships. James Losh was a committed reformer who had, like Wordsworth, witnessed the French Revolution at first hand. Basil Montagu, an illegitimate son of the fourth Earl of Sandwich, was also of a radical persuasion, and later said that meeting Wordsworth had been 'the most fortunate event of my life'. Recently widowed, he was struggling to earn a living as a lawyer while bringing up a young son, also called Basil. Through Montagu, Wordsworth met a liberal clergyman, Francis Wrangham, and two brothers, John Frederick and Azariah Pinney, the sons of a wealthy sugar merchant. The Pinneys, like Raisley Calvert, seem to have sensed potential greatness in Wordsworth, and they made him a generous proposal: they offered him, and Dorothy, their father's little-used house in Dorset, Racedown Lodge. It was arranged, furthermore, that they would live there rent-free, and that they would, for £50 a year, look after Montagu's son Basil. It was to be a turning point in Wordsworth's life.

Racedown: 1795−7

In August Wordsworth travelled ahead to Racedown, stopping at Bristol on the way, and for five weeks enjoyed the city's thriving intellectual life. He met Joseph Cottle, a Unitarian publisher and bookseller, and through him two radical young poets, Robert Southey and Samuel Taylor Coleridge, then causing a stir in the city with a series of public lectures. Coleridge, in particular, impressed him: 'I wished indeed to have seen more [of him]' he wrote to Matthews, 'his talent appears to me very great'. He was presently joined in Bristol by Dorothy, and four days later they and little Basil Montagu took the fifty-mile journey south to Racedown.

Racedown Lodge was a roomy Georgian house close to Lyme Regis in Dorset. It was a beautiful spot, and Wordsworth and Dorothy were soon taking daily morning walks over the neighbouring hills. It was, however, rather remote, and that first winter their only diversions, wrote Dorothy, were 'books, solitude and the fire side'; yet, she insisted, 'I may safely say we are never dull'. In the new year there was a welcome visit from the ebullient Pinney brothers. During the day, Wordsworth joined them in their energetic outdoor pursuits: walking, riding, hunting and chopping wood. In the evening, everyone would gather by the fireside and talk. The Pinneys stayed at Racedown until March. 'I have since *returned* to my books' Wordsworth wrote to Matthews, but otherwise he had little else to report: 'Our present life is utterly barren of such events as merit even the short-lived chronicle of an accidental letter. We plant cabbages, and if retirement, in its full perfection, be as powerful in working transformations as on of Ovid's Gods, you may perhaps suspect that into cabbages we shall be transformed'.

But things were about to change. Azariah Pinney had left Racedown with the manuscript of the revised 'Salisbury Plain', and had given it to Joseph Cottle in Bristol. Cottle, in turn, had passed it on to Coleridge, who had known and admired Wordsworth's poetry since his days as an undergraduate at

The only likeness of Dorothy Wordsworth as a
young woman, by an unknown artist, c.1806.

Cambridge. 'Salisbury Plain' interested him so much that he interleaved the manuscript with blank sheets of paper to allow him to write extensive notes. He was confident that the poem could be published, and he and Wordsworth began to correspond. By the spring, Coleridge was describing Wordsworth as 'a very dear friend', and 'the best poet of the age'. Eager to share his enthusiasm, he sent 'Salisbury Plain' to his friend Charles Lamb in London, who soon reported that he had read the poem 'not without delight'. Encouraged, no doubt, by Coleridge's admiration, Wordsworth began to write with greater energy. By the autumn he was, in Dorothy's words, 'ardent in the composition of a tragedy', 'The Borderers'.

*Samuel Taylor Coleridge, after an original
portrait by Peter Vandyke, 1795.*

At the end of 1796 Mary Hutchinson came to Racedown
and stayed for seven months. Only a few days after her departure Coleridge arrived. Neither Wordsworth or Dorothy ever
forgot the dramatic nature of his entrance. As he approached
the house by the long, curving road, Coleridge caught sight
of the Wordsworths in their orchard. Such was his eagerness
to greet them that he left the road, leapt over a gate, jumped
over a stream, and bounded across a field towards them. To
Dorothy he made an overwhelming impression: 'His conversation teems with soul, mind and spirit', she wrote to Mary
Hutchinson, 'Then he is so benevolent, so good tempered and
cheerful, and, like William, interests himself so much about every little trifle … His eye is large and full … it speaks every

William Wordsworth, after an original
portrait by Robert Hancock, 1798.

emotion of his animated mind; it has more of the "poet's eye in
a fine frenzy rolling" than I have ever witnessed'.

Coleridge was two years younger than Wordsworth, but
had already crammed a remarkable amount into his life. In 1791
he had entered Cambridge University, but after a brilliant start
had begun to drink heavily and had fallen into debt. In 1793
he had enlisted briefly in the 18th Light Dragoons (as Silas
Tomkyn Comberbache), returned to Cambridge, then left at
the end of the year without taking a degree. The following year
he and a friend, Robert Southey, had hatched a short-lived
scheme, 'Pantisocracy', to form an ideal community in New
England, and in 1795 they had lectured in Bristol to raise the
necessary funds. In October that year Coleridge had married

Sara Fricker, and a son, Hartley, had been born in 1796. He had also started a radical journal, *The Watchman*, and published a volume of poetry, *Poems on Various Subjects*. At the end of 1796, after abandoning Pantisocracy, Coleridge had moved his family to Nether Stowey, a small village at the foot of the Quantock Hills in Somerset, some thirty miles north of Racedown.

The sympathy between the two poets was immediate, and their admiration for each other wholehearted; 'Wordsworth is a great man', Coleridge wrote simply to John Prior Estlin. They lost no time in reading their poetry to each other. 'The first thing that was read after he [Coleridge] came was William's new poem *The Ruined Cottage*', Dorothy told Mary Hutchinson, 'with which he was much delighted; and after tea he repeated to us two and a half acts of his tragedy *Osorio*; The next morning William read his tragedy *The Borderers*'.

Alfoxden: 1797–8

At the end of June 1797 Coleridge returned to Nether Stowey. Four days later, the Wordsworths followed after him. Coleridge's home was a tiny, run-down cottage on the western edge of the village. There, with his wife Sara and baby son Hartley, he lived a deliberately simple life: he read, wrote, and kept pigs. His closest friend in the village was Thomas Poole, the owner of the local tannery. Poole was well-known in Bristol for his democratic opinions, and immediately impressed Wordsworth as a kind and considerate employer. 'During my residence at Alfoxden', Wordsworth said many years later, 'I used to see much of him [Poole] and had frequent occasions to admire the conduct of his daily life, especially his conduct to his labourers and poor neighbours … he felt for all men as his brothers'.

'There is everything here' Dorothy enthused to Mary Hutchinson, 'sea, woods wild as fancy ever painted, brooks clear and pebbly as in Cumberland, villages so romantic … Walks extend for miles over the hilltops; the great beauty of which is their wild simplicity'. Wanting to be close to Coleridge,

Alfoxden Park and the Quantocks, by Coplestone Warre Bampfylde.

Wordsworth and Dorothy set about looking for nearby accommodation. Fortunately, they did not have to look for long. On one of their walks they came across Alfoxden House, a large property four miles from Nether Stowey. It was ideal: fully furnished, close to the sea, and within easy walking distance from Coleridge. With Poole's help they obtained a one-year lease, and in July moved in. To celebrate their arrival, Wordsworth and Dorothy held a large dinner party. There were fourteen guests, including the writer and orator John Thelwall, who was staying with the Coleridges at Nether Stowey. Thelwall was a notorious radical, and his presence among a group of people who took strange moonlit walks and who had no obvious employment aroused local suspicions. The country was living in fear of a French invasion, and people were on the lookout for spies. Accordingly, a Home Office agent, a Mr Walsh, was dispatched to investigate. Walsh questioned servants and neighbours, and concluded that though they were not French spies, the inhabitants of Alfoxden House were nevertheless 'a mischievous gang of disaffected Englishmen', and 'a Sett of violent Democrats'.

In truth, agitation was the last thing on anyone's mind. Thelwall's spirit had been broken by constant, often violent resistance to his activities. He had come to south-west England in search of peace; the attraction of the area, he said, was that it enabled him to forget 'all the jarrings and conflicts of the wide world'. Coleridge later recalled one telling moment: 'We were once sitting in a beautiful recess in the Quantocks, when I said to him, "Citizen John, this is a fine place to talk treason in!" – "Nay! Citizen Samuel," replied he, " it is rather a place to make a man forget that there is any necessity for treason!"'.

Wordsworth and Coleridge were also losing interest in direct political activity. Increasingly, their delight was in rural retirement, and in each other's company. The journal that Dorothy kept at Alfoxden shows that she, Wordsworth and Coleridge were in almost daily contact. Their greatest passion was poetry, and in November 1797 Wordsworth and Coleridge embarked upon an extraordinary period of creativity. That month Coleridge composed 'Kubla Khan', the visionary poem which, he later claimed, was written under the influence of opium, a drug commonly taken as a painkiller. Then, on a walking tour along the coast, Wordsworth and Coleridge came up with the idea for 'The Rime of the Ancient Mariner'. It began as a collaboration, but soon Coleridge was writing alone. He worked hard over the winter, and in March 1798 read the completed poem to the Wordsworths. By this time, Wordsworth had himself begun to write in earnest. He had returned to a poem from his Racedown days, 'The Ruined Cottage', which told the story of Margaret, and her slow, painful decline after her husband leaves her to enlist in the army. He developed this 'tale of silent suffering' into one of consolation. He now found, in Margaret's persistent hope, an enduring strength: her ruined cottage became a place of tranquillity, living evidence of 'That secret spring of humanity / Which, mid the calm oblivious tendencies / Of Nature, mid her plants, her weeds and flowers, / And silent overgrowings, still survived.'

As Wordsworth grew more confident, Coleridge remained unstinting in his admiration and encouragement: 'I have known him [Wordsworth] a year and some months', he wrote to his friend Estlin, 'and my admiration, I might say my awe, of his intellectual powers has increased even to this hour, and (what is of more importance) he is a tried good man'. Wordsworth's destiny, as far as Coleridge was concerned, was to be the greatest philosophical poet of the age, and that spring he almost certainly inspired the grand scheme that was to haunt Wordsworth for the rest of his life. In the first week of March Wordsworth told his friend James Tobin that he was busy with a poem 'in which I continue to convey most of the knowledge of which I am possessed … I known not anything which will not come within the scope of my plan'. Five days later he told James Losh: 'I have written 1300 lines of a poem which I hope to make of considerable utility. Its title will be *The Recluse; or Views of Nature, Man and Society*'. For the moment, however, these thirteen hundred lines, which may be a reference to 'The Ruined Cottage', were as far as Wordsworth was to get with 'The Recluse'. Instead, he started to write verse of a very different kind.

The poetry that Wordsworth now turned to was revolutionary. Its subject was the lives and feelings of people who up till then had not been considered at all poetic: the very poor, the very young, the deranged; tinkers, shepherds and huntsmen. And it employed the simplest, most unadorned language. One poem followed another in a period of astonishing invention: 'Goody Blake and Harry Gill', 'The Idiot Boy', 'We are Seven', 'The Thorn', 'Peter Bell', 'Simon Lee' and 'The Mad Mother' all date from this period. 'His faculties seem to expand every day', Dorothy told Mary Hutchinson, 'he composes with much more facility than he did, as to the *mechanism* of poetry, and his ideas flower faster than he can express them'. Years later Wordsworth himself recalled this magical spring, 'wherein we first / Together wandered in wild poesy'.

A portrait of William Hazlitt by William Bewick, 1824.

In May, the young writer William Hazlitt came to Nether Stowey. In a magnificent essay written over twenty years later, *On My First Acquaintance with Poets*, he vividly recalled his introduction both to Wordsworth's poetry – 'the sense of a new style and a new spirit in poetry came over me' – and to Wordsworth himself. It is one of the finest of all descriptions of the poet:

> I think I see him now. He answered in some degree to his friend's description of him, but was more gaunt and Don Quixote-like. He was quaintly dressed (according to the costume of that unconstrained period) in a brown fustian jacket and striped pantaloons. There was something of a roll, a lounge in his gait, not unlike his own Peter Bell. There was a severe, worn pressure of thought about his temples, a fire in his eye (as if he saw something in objects more than outward appearance) an intense, high narrow forehead, a Roman nose, cheeks furrowed by strong purpose and feeling, and a convulsive inclination to laughter about the mouth, a good deal at variance with the solemn, stately expression of the rest of his features … He sat down and talked very naturally and freely, with a mixture of clear, gushing accents in his voice, a deep guttural intonation, a strong tincture of northern *burr*, like the crust on wine. He instantly began to make havoc of the half of Cheshire cheese on the table …

By this time the Wordsworths' tenancy of Alfoxden was running out. There was, however, a plan that would keep everyone together: Wordsworth, Dorothy and Coleridge would all go to Germany, where, Wordsworth told Losh, 'we purpose to pass the two ensuing years in order to acquire the German language, and to furnish ourselves with a tolerable stock of information in natural science. Our plan is to settle, if possible, in a village near a university, in a pleasant, and, if we can, a mountainous, country'. The weeks leading up to the departure for Germany were eventful. At the end of the June Wordsworth and Dorothy vacated Alfoxden and moved to Bristol. On 10 July she and Wordsworth went on a walking tour of the Wye Valley. It was a welcome break from the city, and, for Wordsworth, a reminder of a previous summer, five years before, when he had walked the same paths along the Wye, alone and in very different circumstances. Then he had been restless and anxious. Now, in Dorothy's company, he was inspired to write his greatest poem to date. 'Lines written a few miles above Tintern Abbey' is an expression of Wordsworth's new-found faith in nature, in human passions, and the power of the imagination. It is both a celebration of the last year in Somerset, and its magnificent conclusion.

After four days in the Wye valley, Wordsworth and Dorothy returned to Bristol. They were just in time to include 'Tintern Abbey' in the volume that Wordsworth was now publishing in collaboration with Coleridge: *Lyrical Ballads and other Poems*. Now seen as one of the key publications of the Romantic period, at the time it was chiefly an attempt to raise funds for the German trip. Coleridge contributed 'The Rime of the Ancient Mariner' and four other pieces; the rest of the poems were by Wordsworth. *Lyrical Ballads* was, at Coleridge's insistence, published anonymously: 'Wordsworth's name is nothing', he told Joseph Cottle, the publisher, 'to a large number of people mine *stinks*'. In a preface Wordsworth described the poems as 'experiments', written 'chiefly with a view to ascertain how far the language of conversation in the middle and lower classes of society is adapted to the purposes of poetic pleasure'.

Lyrical Ballads was printed in or around the first week of September. Later that month Wordsworth, Dorothy and Coleridge, together with John Chester, a friend of Coleridge's from Nether Stowey, set sail from Yarmouth.

Germany and the North East: 1798–9

On 18 September, after a rough passage across the North Sea, the party reached the mouth of the river Elbe, and the following day arrived at Hamburg. Coleridge was enthralled by the unfamiliar sights and sounds of the city; Dorothy, on the

A view of Tintern Abbey by Francis Nicholson, c.1804.

other hand, was disgusted by Hamburg's 'dirty, ill-paved stink-
ing streets'. Wordsworth summed up his feelings to Thomas
Poole: 'It is a *sad* place, in this epithet you have the soul and
essence of all the information which I have been able to gather'. After two weeks in the city the Wordsworths and Coleridge
separated. Coleridge was eager to learn German and study the

near & the [illegible]
gay sights of ladies & courtesies whirling along the
I will I will transcribe some lines which are [illegible] ...
slide of course will be interesting to you now. [illegible] pleasures

And in the frosty season when the sun
Was set, and visible for many a mile
The cottage windows through the twilight blazed,
I heeded not the summons: clear and loud
The village clock tolled six, & wheeled about
Proud and exulting like an untired horse
That cares not for his home. All shod with steel
We hissed along the polished ice in games
Confederate, imitative of the chace
And woodland pleasures, the resounding horn,
The pack loud bellowing & the hunted hare.
So through the darkness and the cold we flew
And not a voice was idle: with the din
Meanwhile the precipices [illegible] loud,
The leafless trees and every [illegible] hills
Tinkled like iron, while the [illegible]
Into the tumult sent an [illegible] stars,
Of melancholy, not unnoticed while the [illegible]
Eastward, were sparkling clear, & in the west
The orange sky of evening died away.
Not seldom from the uproar I retired
Into a silent bay, or sportively
Gla[illegible] sideways leaving the tumultuous throng
To cut across the shadow of a star
That gleamed upon the ice. And oftentimes
When we had given our bodies to the winds
And all the shadowy banks on either side
Came sweeping through the darkness, spinning still
The rapid line of motion, then at once
Have I, reclining back upon my heels,
Stopped short; yet still the solitary cliffs
Wheeled by me, even as if the earth had rolled
With visible motion her diurnal round:
Behind me did they stretch in solemn train
Feebler & feebler, & I stood & watched
Till all was tranquil as a summer sea &c

I will give you [crossed out] a Lake Scene of another k[ind]
the map of what [illegible] has written because it [illegible]
from the rest, & because you have now a Lake daily b[efore]

great German philosophers, and left for the fashionable town of Ratzeburgh some thirty miles to the east. Wordsworth and Dorothy, lacking Coleridge's clarity of purpose, and financially much more constrained, decided to pass the winter in Goslar, a town two hundred miles to the south, at the foot of the Hartz Mountains in Lower Saxony. It seemed a good choice, for Goslar boasted a distinguished history, and had the great advantage of being cheap, but when they arrived there the Wordsworths were disappointed. Badly damaged over the years by fire and war, Goslar turned out to be no more than a dull provincial town – 'once the residence of Kings, now the residence of Grocers and Linen-drapers' wrote Wordsworth to Thomas Poole.

Wordsworth and Dorothy stayed in Goslar for five lonely months. The worst winter of the century allowed them only the briefest of daily walks, and so most of their time was spent indoors. Isolated, and intensely homesick, Wordsworth withdrew into himself. His thoughts turned to the Lake District, and to his earliest childhood memories: the music of the River Derwent as it flowed along the bottom of his garden in Cockermouth; skating on Esthwaite Water; and how, one moonlit night, he had stolen a shepherd's boat and rowed out on to Ullswater. Inspired by the conviction that it was in these early experiences that he would find the foundations for his creative adult life, Wordsworth began to shape his thoughts into verse, and so began, in its earliest form, his great autobiographical poem, *The Prelude*. It was an intense, exhausting process: in a letter Wordsworth complained to Coleridge of 'an uneasiness at my stomach and side, with a dull pain about my heart … I am absolutely consumed by thinking and feeling'.

In February the winter began to abate, and Wordsworth and Dorothy were keen to depart. They left Goslar at the end of the month, and spent the next few weeks rambling through the Hartz Mountains. In April they arrived at the ancient university town of Göttingen, where Coleridge was now living. They had missed each other keenly, and it was an emotional reunion, but Coleridge noticed that Wordsworth was full of 'impatience to return to their native country'. Within a week Wordsworth and Dorothy were back in Hamburg, and by the end of April they had reached England, after nearly eight months abroad.

Almost immediately they proceeded north to Sockburn-on-Tees in County Durham, the home of Mary Hutchinson and her family. In July Coleridge returned from Germany, and in October, together with Joseph Cottle, he arrived at Sockburn. Five days after his arrival, he, Cottle and Wordsworth set out for a three-week walking tour of the Lake District. Soon after their departure, at Greta Bridge, Cottle broke off and returned to London. But further on, at Temple Sowerby near the north east border of the Lake District, Wordsworth and Coleridge were joined by Wordsworth's sailor brother John, then enjoying a rare break from the sea. Together they entered the Lake District from the north, walking south through Kentmere to Troutbeck and Hawkshead. From there they proceeded north through the central fells to Ambleside and Grasmere. At Grisedale John Wordsworth left them, while Wordsworth and Coleridge continued north to Keswick. The second part of their journey took them to the wilder lakes in the west: Buttermere, Ennerdale and Wastwater. Finally, they looped back to the north east, ending up at Pooley Bridge on the northern shore of Ullswater. Here they visited the anti-Slave Trade campaigner, Thomas Clarkson, and his wife Catherine, who was considerably impressed by Wordsworth: 'Wordsworth has a fine commanding figure', she wrote, 'is rather handsome & looks as if he was born to be a great Prince or a great General. He seems very fond of C[oleridge] laughing at all his jokes & taking all opportunities of showing him off & to crown all he has the manners of a gentleman'.

This tour, which took them through the heart of the Lakes, was to have a momentous effect on both poets. For Coleridge, it was an overwhelming introduction to a new kind of landscape:

A view of Grasmere by John White Abbott, 1791.

'how deeply I have been impressed by a world of scenery absolutely new to me', he wrote afterwards to Dorothy, 'It was to me a vision of a fair Country'. For Wordsworth, it heralded a return to his native soil. At Grasmere he had seen a small cottage available for rent, and separating from Coleridge at Pooley Bridge he returned there to arrange a lease. In December he and Dorothy left Sockburn for Grasmere. After a dramatic winter journey through the Yorkshire Dales they reached Kendal, where they bought furniture. On the evening of 20 December they arrived in Grasmere.

Grasmere: 1799–1808

In October 1769 the poet Thomas Gray had passed through Grasmere, and described the valley in his journal: 'Not a single red tile, no flaring gentleman's house, or garden walls, break in upon the repose of this little unsuspected paradise; but all is peace, rusticity, and happy poverty, in its neatest, most becoming attire'. Some years later, Wordsworth had, as a schoolboy, walked to Grasmere from Hawkshead. He too had thought it a paradise. Now he was fulfilling this childhood

Dove Cottage and Town End by Dora Wordsworth.

dream. 'Embrace me, then, ye Hills, and close me in' he wrote in 'Home at Grasmere', a poem he began soon after his arrival. He had come to 'this sublime retirement' to write poetry. Here he could dedicate himself to the great task of writing 'The Recluse'.

Wordsworth's and Dorothy's new home, now known as Dove Cottage, was a small lakeland dwelling dating from the sixteenth century. It was one of the handful of cottages and farm buildings that made up Town End, a hamlet just outside Grasmere village itself. The life Wordsworth and Dorothy led there was frugal and committed. It was also, from the very beginning, a life they shared with others. The first to arrive was Wordsworth's brother John. He came at the end of January 1800, and stayed until the end of September. John was a reticent man, but deeply sensitive to all around him. To Wordsworth he was a 'silent Poet' who possessed 'a watchful heart' and 'an eye practised like a blind man's touch'. John fitted easily into their lives; he had, Dorothy wrote, 'a perfect sympathy with all our pleasures'. Mary Hutchinson came in late February, and stayed for six weeks. Immediately after her departure,

Coleridge arrived. He did not, on this occasion, stay long, returning to Nether Stowey the following month, but in June he
was back again, this time to stay. He, Sara and Hartley went to
live at Greta Hall in Keswick, twelve miles to the north. The
Alfoxden group was together again, and, undeterred by the
twelve mile walk between Grasmere and Keswick, Wordsworth
and Coleridge were continual visitors to each other's homes
over the coming months.

In May 1800 Dorothy began a journal, and continued
it for the next two and a half years. As one reads it now, the
Wordsworths' day-to-day existence at Dove Cottage comes to
life. Dorothy records everything, from the reading and writing
of poetry to the smallest domestic details. She records her and
Wordsworth's exchanges with the local inhabitants and their
chance meetings with travellers, vagrants and solitaries on the
road; she records the visitors to the cottage, and their daily activities of walking, gardening, fishing and boating. Private and
intimate, intended only for herself and her brother, Dorothy's
journal captures the intense emotions of the first years at Dove
Cottage. It also reveals Dorothy's skill as a descriptive writer.
At Nether Stowey, Coleridge had remarked upon her talent for
observation: 'Her eye watchful in minutest observation of nature; and her taste a perfect electrometer. It bends, protrudes,
and draws in, at subtlest beauties and most recondite faults'.

Coleridge and Wordsworth were now planning a second
edition of *Lyrical Ballads*. The book appeared at the beginning of the following year, in two volumes. The first volume
contained, reordered and somewhat revised, the poems from
the first edition. The second volume was largely made up of
new poems written by Wordsworth during his first year at Dove
Cottage, including 'Lucy Gray', 'The Two April Mornings',
'The Fountain', 'The Old Cumberland Beggar', 'The Brothers'
and 'Michael'. The last two poems are among Wordsworth's
finest works, and are concerned with the Lake District 'statesmen', owners of small estates who lived an independent life

among the hills. In presenting a copy of *Lyrical Ballads* to the politician Charles James Fox Wordsworth wrote that the two poems 'were written with a view to shew that men who do not wear fine cloaths can feel deeply'.

The second edition of *Lyrical Ballads* contained a lengthy preface. Here Wordsworth first articulated the theories of poetry that he and Coleridge had been developing since the days in Somerset. The poems of *Lyrical Ballads* were written, he explained, 'to make the incidents of common life interesting by tracing in them, truly though not ostentatiously, the primary laws of our nature: chiefly as far as regards the manner in which we associate ideas in a state of excitement'. Poetry he defined as 'the spontaneous overflow of powerful feelings: it takes its origin from emotion recollected in tranquillity'.

The second year at Dove Cottage was quieter than the first. There is a gap in Dorothy's journal from December 1800 to October 1801, and Wordsworth wrote little. In the spring, John Wordsworth, now captain of the merchant ship the *Earl of Abergavenny*, departed for a lengthy voyage. Coleridge was ill for much of the year, and in November left the Lake District to winter in the south. At the beginning of 1802 Wordsworth and Mary Hutchinson became engaged.

The new year also brought fresh composition. Wordsworth was again revising 'The Ruined Cottage', now known as 'The Pedlar'. He was also writing new poetry: 'Alice Fell', 'Beggars' and 'To H.C., Six Years Old', a poem to Hartley Coleridge. At the end of March, over breakfast, he began one of his greatest poems, 'Ode. Intimations of Immortality from Recollections of Early Childhood'. In May he started another major poem, known amongst family and friends as 'The Leech Gatherer', but later published as 'Resolution and Independence'. In October 1800 he and Dorothy had encountered an old man by the road who, they were dismayed to discover, had lost nine of his ten children. His trade, Dorothy wrote had written in her journal, 'was to gather leeches but now leeches were scarce &

& at last under the boughs
of the trees, we saw that there
was a long belt of them
~~along~~ along the
shore, about the breadth
of a country turnpike road.
I never saw daffodils so
beautiful they grew among
the mossy stones about & about
them, some rested their heads
upon these stones as on a
pillow for weariness & the
rest tossed & reeled & danced
& seemed as if they verily
laughed with the wind that blew
upon them over the lake, they
looked so gay ever glancing
ever changing. This wind blew directly over the lake to them
here & there a little knot
and a few stragglers a few
yards higher up but they
were so few as not to disturb

Entry from Dorothy's Journal: Daffodils by Thirlmere.

he had not strength for it – he lived by begging & was making his way to Carlisle where he should buy a few godly books to sell'. Now, almost two years later, Wordsworth returned to this memorable encounter, finding in it an example of supreme fortitude and human dignity in the face of adversity.

That summer, the Peace of Amiens brought a truce between England and France. It was an unexpected opportunity for Wordsworth to see Annette Vallon and, for the first time, his daughter Caroline, and in July he and Dorothy left Dove Cottage for France. At the beginning of August they arrived in Calais, where they had arranged to meet Annette and Caroline. In the evenings they would all walk along the shore and talk, but here Dorothy's journal falls silent, and we know nothing of what passed between them.

Wordsworth and Dorothy arrived back in England in September, and headed straight for the Hutchinsons' home in the north east. On 4 October, at 8 o'clock in the morning, Wordsworth and Mary Hutchinson were married. Immediately after the wedding breakfast, Wordsworth, Mary and Dorothy began the journey back to Dove Cottage. Mary's calm, self-effacing presence, and the domestic tranquillity that came with it, sustained Wordsworth for the rest of his life. 'It does a man's heart good, I will not say, to know such a family', commented Coleridge, 'but even – to know that there is such a Family … [Wordsworth's] is the happiest Family, I ever saw'.

Coleridge's own life, by contrast, was now in serious decline. Plagued by ill health, he had turned to opium for relief, and was now addicted to the drug. His marriage was failing, and he had developed a hopeless, obsessive love for Mary Hutchinson's sister Sara. In April he wrote his 'Letter to Sara Hutchinson', in which he brooded upon his unhappiness and the decline of his creative powers. Later in the month he read the poem to the Wordsworths: 'Coleridge came to us and repeated the verses he wrote to Sara', wrote Dorothy, 'I was affected with them & was on the whole, not being well, in miserable spirits'.

In June 1803 Wordsworth's first child, John, was born. Two months later Wordsworth, Coleridge and Dorothy set off for a tour of Scotland. If this was an attempt to reunite the old Alfoxden group then it failed. Signs of strain soon began to show. Coleridge apparently found Wordsworth 'hypochondriacal … silent and self-centered', and after only two weeks he and the Wordsworths continued north separately. Wordsworth and Dorothy reached as far north as Glencoe and Killiecrankie in the Scottish Highlands, then returned through the Trossachs, Linlithgow, Edinburgh and Melrose, arriving back at Grasmere in late September. Dorothy recalled their six-week tour in her *Recollections of a Tour made in Scotland*, while a number a Wordsworth's best-known poems derive from this trip, including 'Stepping Westward' and 'The Solitary Reaper'.

Wordsworth forged a vital new friendship this year. In either July or August he met Sir George Beaumont in Keswick. Beaumont was a wealthy landowner; more importantly he was a patron and lover of the arts, and a distinguished amateur artist himself. Beaumont's circle of friends included the artists Sir Thomas Lawrence, John Constable, David Wilkie and Benjamin West, but even in this distinguished company Wordsworth seems to have made a particular impression, for Beaumont made the poet a remarkably generous gift – a parcel of land at Applethwaite, near Keswick. Over the coming years he and Lady Beaumont would prove to be the most faithful of friends, and tireless advocates of Wordsworth's poetry.

At the end of the year Coleridge arrived at Dove Cottage. By now, the extent of his decline was painfully apparent. 'I must tell you about Coleridge', Dorothy wrote to Catherine Clarkson in January 1804, 'two or three days before [he] was lame with the gout, stomach-sick, haunted by ugly dreams, screamed out in the night, durst not sleep etc etc …' That March, in a final bid to rescue his health, Coleridge sailed to Malta. The Wordsworths were not to see him again for another two years.

In the weeks leading up to Coleridge's departure, Dorothy and Mary had busily copied all Wordsworth's unpublished poems into a notebook, 'to be his companions in Italy'. Throughout this last year Wordsworth had been producing new poetry at an astonishing rate. He had finished the 'Ode. Intimations of Immortality', written the 'Ode to Duty', and composed perhaps his most famous poem, 'I wandered lonely as a cloud'. Above all, he had returned to the autobiographical verses begun years ago at Goslar. In 1799 he had composed a two-part version of the poem, now known to us as *The Prelude*, but then referred to simply as the 'Poem to Coleridge'. In Grasmere he expanded this into a much more ambitious work. His theme, intended as a introduction to 'The Recluse', was nothing less than the growth of his own mind. In magnificently assured verse Wordsworth traced the guiding forces that had shaped his adult life: from his childhood in Cockermouth and schooldays in Esthwaite, to Cambridge and the Alps, Wales, London, and revolutionary France. By the spring of 1804 Wordsworth had completed a five-book version of the poem.

In August Wordsworth's second second child, a daughter, was born. Christened Dorothy, she was always known to the family as Dora. 'She is her Father's darling', Dorothy wrote to Lady Beaumont in September, 'She wins her way into all our hearts'. But the following year their happiness gave way to sorrow. On 5 February 1805 John Wordsworth's ship, the *Earl of Abergavenny*, had struck rocks off Portland Bill on the Dorset coast, and had sunk during the night. Fewer than half of the 387 passengers and crew had survived, and John Wordsworth, who stayed at his command, had not been among them. The news of his death came to the family at Grasmere like 'a thunderstroke'. 'For myself', Wordsworth wrote, 'I feel that there is something cut out of my life which cannot be restored'. In May, Wordsworth completed a final, thirteen-book version of *The Prelude*. It was his finest achievement, but all he felt was dejection. 'It was not a happy day for me', he confessed to Sir

And, after ordinary Travellers talk
With our Conductor, we sank
Each into commerce with his private thoughts
Thus did we breast the ascent, and by myself
Was nothing either seen or heard the while
Which took me from my musings, save that once
The Shepherd's cur did to his own great joy
Unearth a hedge-hog in the mountain crags
Round which he made a barking turbulent.
This small adventure, (for even such it seem'd
In that wild place and at the dead of night)
Being over and forgotten, on we wound
In silence as before. With forehead bent
Earthward, as if in opposition set
Against an enemy, I panted up
With eager pace, and no less eager thoughts.
Thus might we wear a midnight hour away,
Ascending at loose distance each from each,
And I, as chanced, the foremost of the Band,
When at my feet the ground appear'd to brighten,
And with a step or two seem'd brighter still,
Nor was I time given to ask the cause,
For instantly a Light upon the turf
Fell like a flash; I look'd up, and lo
The Moon stood naked in the Heavens, at height
Immense above my head, and on the shore
Of a huge sea, in clear and open air

A page from the original manuscript of the 1805 Prelude.

George Beaumont a fortnight later, 'when I looked back upon the performance it seemed to have a dead weight about it, the reality so far short of the expectation … above all, many heavy thoughts of my poor departed Brother hung upon me; the joy which I should have had in shewing him the Manuscript and a thousand other vain fancies and dreams'.

Grasmere: 1806–12

The memory of John continued to haunt Wordsworth. In April and May 1806 he was in London. There he met the Whig leader Charles James Fox and the artists Joseph Farington, David Wilkie and James Northcote. He had his portrait taken by the fashionable portrait painter Henry Edridge. But he spent most of his time with Sir George and Lady Beaumont at their home in Grosvenor Square, and there he saw a picture by Beaumont, *Peele Castle in a Storm*, which again brought to mind John's death. The poem he was then inspired to write, the great 'Elegiac Stanzas', finds, amidst grief, a kind of consolation. At the end of May Wordsworth was back in Grasmere, and shortly after his return his third child, Thomas, was born. Life at Dove Cottage, from a practical point of view, was becoming difficult. As many as nine people now had to live and sleep in its half-dozen rooms. In 1804, after Dora's birth, Dorothy had described the cottage as 'sadly crowded'. Now, she said, they were 'crammed in our little nest edge full … Every bed lodges two persons at present'. Fortunately, a temporary solution offered itself in the autumn, when the Beaumonts invited the Wordsworths to winter at their country estate, Coleorton, in Leicestershire.

On 26 October 1806 the entire family left Dove Cottage for Leicestershire. On the first night of their journey, in Kendal, they had a long wished-for, but ultimately upsetting reunion. Coleridge had returned to England in August, but had delayed his journey north for two months. Now, after the long separation, the Wordsworths found a figure they barely recognised.

'We all went thither to him', wrote Dorothy, 'and never did I feel such a shock as at first sight of him. His fatness has quite changed him – it is more like the flesh of a person in a dropsy than one in health; his eyes are lost in it'. In conversation they found Coleridge reserved and impersonal, continually changing the subject 'to anything but what we were yearning after'. They invited Coleridge to join them in Leicestershire, which he did, with his son Hartley, in December.

The Wordsworths were at Coleorton for almost eight months. Beaumont was rebuilding the main house, and had asked Wordsworth to design a new winter garden. In the last few years Wordsworth had transformed the garden at Dove Cottage, and this was an opportunity for him to exercise his considerable skills as a gardener. In the evenings, the family gathered by the fireside, and Wordsworth read them lines from *The Prelude*. Coleridge – by now, according to Dorothy, 'much more like his own old self' – was overwhelmed by the poem.

While he was at Coleorton Wordsworth also worked on his first publication since the second edition of *Lyrical Ballads*. That winter and spring the whole household, including Coleridge, helped him prepare his new volume of poetry for the press, and in April 1807 *Poems, in Two Volumes* was published. It contained the best of Wordsworth's later poems at Dove Cottage. Alongside a multitude of exquisite lyrics are some of his finest works: the 'Sonnets dedicated to Liberty' written in 1802 after his return from Calais; 'Resolution and Independence', 'Ode to Duty', the 'Immortality Ode', 'Elegiac Stanzas', in all over a hundred new poems. But the reviews were, almost without exception, hostile. 'A more rash and injudicious speculation on the weakness or the depravity of the public taste has seldom been made', wrote James Montgomery in the *Eclectic Review*. Byron called the poetry 'namby-pamby', and Francis Jeffrey, in the *Edinburgh Review*, condemned Wordsworth's rustic subject matter as 'low, silly, or uninteresting'. 'My flesh is as insensible as iron to these petty stings',

Wordsworth declared to Lady Beaumont, but he was, in truth, discouraged from publishing anything else for several years.

The Wordsworths arrived back in Grasmere in July 1807. That winter, the cottage received one of its last visitors, the writer Thomas De Quincey. As a seventeen year-old, De Quincey had written an effusive letter of praise to Wordsworth, and in reply had received a polite invitation to come to Grasmere. Now aged twenty-one, he had finally plucked up the courage to accept the offer. Years later, he wrote a wonderful description of his initial impressions of the cottage. He described a 'very prettily wainscotted' front room, with a single window 'with little diamond panes, embowered, at almost every season of the year, with roses; and, in the summer and autumn, with a profusion of jessamine and other fragrant shrubs'. Mary Wordsworth, he wrote, was 'a tall young woman, with the most winning expression of benignity upon her features that I ever beheld', while Dorothy was 'a lady, much shorter, much slighter … Her face was of Egyptian brown; rarely, in a woman of English birth, had I seen a more determinate gipsy tan. Her eyes were not soft, as Mrs. Wordsworth's nor were they fierce and bold, but they were wild and startling, and hurried in their motion'.

It was the family's last winter at Dove Cottage. In May 1808, with great regret, they were forced move to a larger house, Allan Bank, on the other side of the lake. Allan Bank was a large white house standing just above Grasmere village. As a piece of local architecture, Wordsworth despised it. In 1805 he had watched it being built for a Liverpool lawyer, 'a wretched creature … of the name of Crump', and had written to a friend in dismay: 'When you next enter the sweet Paradise of Grasmere you will see staring you in the face, upon that beautiful ridge that elbows out into the vale (behind the church and towering far above its steeple) a temple of abomination … this House will stare you in the face from every part of the Vale, and entirely destroy its character of simplicity and seclusion'. What Allan Bank could provide, however, was space. With a wife and three children,

Grasmere by George Fennel Robson, showing Allan Bank (centre).

a sister, a sister-in-law, and servants, Wordsworth now had a large household, and it was about to become larger still. At the beginning of September Coleridge appeared, and stayed with the Wordsworths, on and off, for the next two years. His young sons, Hartley and Berkeley, went to school in neighbouring Ambleside, and spent their weekends at Allan Bank. Later that month Wordsworth's second daughter, Catherine, was born. Finally, in November, Thomas De Quincey arrived. He became a much-loved addition to the family, and was a great favourite with the children.

For the first year and half at Allan Bank, Wordsworth was largely preoccupied with prose works. He had lost none of his interest in public affairs (indeed, in 1833 he remarked that 'he had given twelve hours' thought to the condition and prospects of society, for one to poetry'), and his first project was a political pamphlet, *The Convention of Cintra*. For several months he thought of little else. Coleridge's daughter Sara, who visited Allan Bank that autumn, later wrote in her *Memoir*: 'How gravely and earnestly used Samuel Taylor Coleridge and William Wordsworth and my uncle Southey also to discuss the affairs of the nation, as if it all came home to their business and bosoms, as if it were their private concern!'

In February 1809 *The Convention of Cintra*, was ready for publication, and De Quincey left for London to see it through the press. Meanwhile Coleridge was busy with a new venture. On 1 June he published the first issue of a weekly periodical, *The Friend, A Literary, Moral and Political Weekly Paper*, written and promoted almost entirely by himself. Wordsworth helped by contributing two substantial pieces to the journal. The first, *Reply to Mathetes*, was a response to a letter in *The Friend* from Alexander Blair and John Wilson (later famous as 'Christopher North' of *Blackwoods* magazine, and a future Professor of Moral Philosophy at Edinburgh University), and concerned itself with the education of the young. The second piece, which appeared in the final issue of *The Friend* on 15 March 1810, was the first of his three *Essays upon Epitaphs*.

One other important prose work dates from Wordsworth's time at Allan Bank. In 1809 a clergyman from the north-east of England, the Reverend Joseph Wilkinson, asked Wordsworth if he would contribute an introduction to a book of engravings made after his own watercolours, *Select Views in Cumberland, Westmorland, and Lancashire*. Wordsworth hesitated at first, as he had a decidedly low opinion of Wilkinson's drawings, but the introduction that he eventually wrote was published in 1810. Over the years, this was to grow and develop until it became one of his best-known (and best-selling) works: *A Guide through the District of the Lakes*. Here, Wordsworth lovingly described his native scenery, and first articulated the idea that the Lake District should be a national park.

All this literary activity could not, however, disguise the fact that by 1810 life at Allan Bank had become extremely difficult. Despite its size, the house was crowded, and Coleridge was moody and withdrawn. In March, Sara Hutchinson, worn out by her constant work on *The Friend*, and made ill by Coleridge's persistent, hopeless devotion, left Allan Bank for her brother Tom's farm in Wales. In May, Coleridge himself left for Keswick. Later that month, Mary gave birth to her fifth and final child, William, and in July Wordsworth and Dorothy travelled south to stay with the Beaumonts at Coleorton. It was a welcome respite, but a brief one, for that autumn the tension between Wordsworth and Coleridge developed into an open quarrel.

At the beginning of September Wordsworth returned north. Later that month he was joined at Allan Bank by Basil Montagu. Montagu had heard of Coleridge's condition, and confidently believed that he could provide him with the 'tranquillity' he needed. Coleridge, still in Keswick, agreed to return with Montagu to London, and in mid October arrived at Allan Bank. After a brief conversation with Wordsworth, he and Montagu proceeded south. In the meantime, however, Wordsworth had tried to convince Montagu that his confidence was misplaced; 'William used many arguments to persuade M. that his purpose of keeping Coleridge comfortable could not be answered by their being in the same house together', Dorothy explained to Catherine Clarkson some time later, 'but in vain … After this William spoke out and told M the nature of C's habits'. Once they were in London, Montagu told Coleridge that he had been 'commissioned' to repeat what Wordsworth had said. According to Coleridge, when he recalled the incident later, this was that he was 'a rotten drunkard' and 'an absolute nuisance to the family', who was 'rotting out his entrails with intemperance'. Coleridge was deeply hurt. It was the start of a long and painful estrangement.

In the summer of 1811 the Wordsworths left Allan Bank, and moved into the rectory next to Grasmere church. After his digression into prose, Wordsworth was again writing poetry, and had returned to 'The Recluse'. For the first time, however, he was unable to share his great work with Coleridge – the two friends were refusing to speak to each other. In February 1812 Coleridge travelled through Grasmere on his way to Keswick, and even then he did not stop and call at the rectory. In May, after Wordsworth had travelled to London 'with a *determination* to confront Coleridge and Montagu upon this vile business', they finally put aside their differences, but the intimacy of earlier years was never to return.

While Wordsworth was in the south, tragedy struck at home. His daughter Catherine had never been strong. In April 1810 she had been siezed by a violent convulsive fit that had left her partly paralysed. Two years later, on the evening of 3 June, Catherine was again siezed by convulsions, and died early the following morning, aged only four. It was almost a week before Wordsworth received the news. Then, in December, the Wordsworths' second son, the six year-old, 'heavenly-tempered' Thomas, died of pneumonia after contracting measles. 'I dare not say in what state of mind I am', Wordsworth wrote to Robert Southey. 'I loved the Boy with all with the utmost love of which my soul is capable, and he is taken from me'.

A year later, the memory of Catherine inspired Wordsworth to write one of his most moving sonnets, 'Surprized by joy – impatient as the Wind'.

Rydal Mount: 1813–33

In the weeks following Thomas's death Wordsworth's one concern was the well-being of his bereaved family. Two things were clear to him. Firstly, he had to achieve some measure of financial security. Secondly, the family had to leave Grasmere. Financial help came soon. Wordsworth's father had worked for the Earl of Lonsdale. Now the earl's heir, Sir William Lowther, once he had learned of the poet's situation, offered him £100 a year until he could find him a salaried position. After some hesitation, Wordsworth accepted this generous offer, 'until the office becomes vacant, or any other change takes place in my circustances which might render it unnecessary'. To his relief, he did not have to wait long: in April 1813, he was appointed Distributor of Stamps for Westmorland and part of Cumberland. As such, he was responsible for collecting the taxes payable on all legal documents created in the district, and

Rydal Mount by William Westall, 1831.

sending them down to the Board of Stamps in London. It was a job he was to perform dilligently for almost thirty years.

This improvement in Wordsworth's fortunes enabled him, at last, to leave the rectory, and in May he and his family moved to the neighbouring village of Rydal. Their new home, Rydal Mount, delighted them. It was roomy and comfortable, and had a clear view over Rydal Water towards Loughrigg Fell. There was a good-sized garden, which they set about developing with their usual skill.

In the summer of 1814 Wordsworth and Mary, together with their son John and Sara Hutchinson, toured Scotland. While he was in Scotland, Wordsworth's latest poem, *The Excursion*, was published. This was his first published poetry since *Poems in Two Volumes* in 1807, and was Miltonic in both its length – almost eight thousand lines of blank verse – and its ambition. It began with a revised version of the poem that Wordsworth had first written at Racedown, 'The Ruined Cottage', and then developed into a long philosophical debate between three principal characters: the Wanderer (philosophical, closely attached to nature); the Solitary (pessimistic, disillusioned); and the Pastor (strong in religious faith). Even physically the book was imposing: a beautifully produced quarto volume highly priced at two guineas.

But if *The Excursion* was Wordsworth's most ambitious work to date, it also announced his wider, still unrealised ambition, 'The Recluse'. *The Excursion* was only 'a portion' of this great work. 'Several years ago', Wordsworth wrote in the preface, 'when the Author retired to his native mountains, in the hope of being enabled to construct a literary work that might live, it was a reasonable thing that he should take a review of his own mind, and examine how far Nature and Education had qualified him for such employment'. This 'review' was the as yet unpublished *Prelude*, and, echoing the letter he had written to Losh sixteen years ago, Wordsworth went on to say that 'the result of the investigation which gave rise to it was a determination to compose a philosophical poem, containing views of Man, Nature and Society; and to be entitled, the Recluse; as having for its principal subject the sensations and opinions of a poet living in retirement'. In an extended metaphor, Wordsworth then described his life's work: taking the form of a gothic church, he saw *The Prelude* as 'the ante-chapel', and *The Excursion* as the 'body'. His many smaller poems, 'minor Pieces, which have been long before the Public', were 'the little cells, or oratories, and sepuchral recesses, ordinarily included in those edifices'. He concluded with a 'Prospectus', part of the poem he had written when he first arrived at Dove Cottage, 'Home at Grasmere'.

A year after *The Excursion* Wordsworth consolidated his poetic achievement so far with two more publications. First, he collected his shorter poetry into two volumes, extensively revised, and arranged not chronologically, but into themes such as 'Poems Founded on the Affections', 'Poems Proceeding from Sentiment and Reflection', and 'Poems referring to the Period of Childhood', thus establishing the idea of a coherent body of work. Then he published a poem originally written in 1808, *The White Doe of Rylestone*. Like *The Excursion* this was a deluxe quarto volume, and it had as its frontispiece an engraving of the poem's setting, Bolton Abbey in Yorkshire, after a picture by Sir George Beaumont, to whom the poem was dedicated. Wordsworth had dedicated *The Excursion* to his new patron, Sir William Lowther.

The Excursion, the *Collected Poems*, and *The White Doe of Rylestone* were Wordsworth's justification for his years of retirement in Grasmere. Together, they comprised his achievement thus far as a poet, and he hoped they would restore his reputation after the failure of *Poems, in Two Volumes*. But critics and his fellow writers were disappointed, and sales were poor. 'This will never do' began Francis Jeffrey in his devastating review of *The Excursion* in the *Edinburgh Review*. 'It is longer, weaker, and tamer, than any of Mr Wordsworth's other productions; with less boldness of originality, and less even of that extreme simplicity and lowliness of tone which wavered so prettily, in the *Lyrical Ballads*, between silliness and pathos'. His review of *The White Doe of Rylestone* was similarly direct: 'This, we think, has the merit of being the very worst poem we ever saw in a quarto volume'. Jeffrey considered Wordsworth a self-indulgent mystic; his exploration of his own life and feelings was egotism, and his choice of rural subjects misguided.

Younger writers felt that Wordsworth (and Coleridge and Southey with him) had betrayed his early radicalism by allying himself with a reactionary Tory government and the established church. They believed that his poetry had suffered as a result. 'Shelley … brings home Wordsworth's Excursion, of which we read a part', Mary Shelley noted in her journal in 1814, 'much disappointed. He is a slave'. Two years later Shelley published a sonnet, 'To Wordsworth', in which he expressed his feeling of betrayal. But for one young poet, John Keats,

William Wordsworth by Benjamin Robert Haydon, 1819.

The Excursion was one of the 'three things to rejoice at in this Age'. In 1816 he sent a sonnet to a friend of Wordsworth's, the historical painter Benjamin Robert Haydon, 'Great spirits on earth now are sojourning', in which he described Wordsworth as 'He of the cloud, the cataract, the lake / Who on Helvellyn's summit wide awake / catches his freshness from Archangel's wing'. He characterized Wordsworth's poetry brilliantly as the 'egotistical sublime', and thought him 'deeper than Milton' in his capacity to 'look into the human heart'.

The following year Wordsworth was publishing again: 'Peter Bell', a poem written at Alfoxden, and 'Benjamin the Waggoner'. The sales of the former benefited from a parody by John Hamilton Reynolds, which had ingeniously contrived to appear before the poem itself. In 1819 he published a sonnet sequence, *The River Duddon*, and for once the reviews were almost universally favourable, and sales good. The last poem in the sequence – 'I thought of Thee, my partner and my guide,' – is justly famous. Shortly after the *Duddon* sonnets came *The Miscellaneous Poems of William Wordsworth*. Here Wordsworth gathered together all the shorter poems he had written up to then, as if clearing the way for his major work, 'The Recluse', but Sara Hutchinson was understandably sceptical: 'he *says* he will never trouble himself with anything but the *Recluse*', she wrote. Wordsworth also reviewed his past in a more personal way. From July to November 1820 he, Mary and Dorothy, made a tour of Europe. They followed, quite deliberately, the steps that Wordsworth had taken through the continent thirty years before with Robert Jones. They also spent a month with Annette and Caroline in Paris. It was the first meeting between Wordsworth's wife and the mother of his first child.

In 1821 Wordworth published *Ecclesiastical Sketches*, a sequence of over a hundred sonnets prompted by the current issue of Catholic Emancipation. Its purpose, wrote Wordsworth, 'was, as much as possible, to confine my view to the introduction, progress and operation of the church in England, both previous and subsequent to the Reformation'. The following year he published a group of poems inspired by his recent trip to Europe, *Memorials of a Tour on the Continent, 1820*, and, for the first time separately, the *Description of the Scenery of the Lakes*.

Over the next ten years, however, Wordsworth wrote little, and published nothing new. Instead, he threw himself into an energetic social life. For most of the coming decade, Rydal

Mount was packed with visitors. When Wordsworth wasn't entertaining, he travelled. London was a favourite destination, for there he could both enjoy high society and see old friends. He also travelled extensively abroad: in 1823 he toured Belgium and Holland; in 1828 he, Dora and Coleridge made, apparently on impulse, a tour of Belgium, the Rhineland and Holland. All this activity left little room for poetry. A new five-volume edition of his works appeared in May 1827, otherwise, he was silent, and sometimes he felt the absence of new poems keenly. 'The Muse has foresaken me', he wrote to Haydon in 1831, 'being scared away by the villainous aspect of the Times'. Hartley Coleridge remarked that as the years passed by, Wordsworth became 'less of the Poet, and more of the respectable, talented, hospitable Country gentleman'.

In August 1831 Wordsworth and Dora visited Walter Scott at his home in Abbotsford. Scott had less than a year to live, and Wordsworth was deeply affected by the sight of his friend and fellow writer, aged and exhausted by debt and overwork: The poem he wrote memorialising that day, 'Yarrow Revisited', has the elegiac dignity that was to distinguish the best of his later work.

Final Years: 1833–50

In the last years of his life Wordsworth finally achieved literary fame. *Yarrow Revisited and other Poems*, published in 1835, was his first genuinely popular work. In 1836–7 he worked on another collected edition of his works, in six volumes, and made his habitual painstaking revisions. The following year *The Sonnets of William Wordsworth* appeared, a deluxe volume containing some 415 examples of Wordsworth's favourite poetic form. His international profile was growing too, and he was particularly popular in America. In his final years Wordsworth also turned, once again, to *The Prelude*. He still considered the poem too personal to be published in his lifetime, but he revised it for publication after his death.

At Rydal Mount Wordsworth began to receive an enormous number of letters, gifts, and requests from unknown admirers and would-be poets. Others were determined to see the famous poet in person. These visitors (and the visitors book kept at Rydal Mount records many hundreds of them) ranged from the distinguished – Queen Adelaide of England, Ralph Waldo Emerson – to the tourist and souvenir hunter. Wordsworth, hardly less than the mountains and lakes themselves, was a part of the landscape.

With fame came official honours. In 1838 Wordsworth received an honorary degree at Durham University. The following year he was made an honorary doctor of civil law at Oxford. Finally, in 1843, following the death of Robert Southey, he was offered the Poet Laureateship. At first Wordsworth refused; he was, he said, too old. But when the prime minister, Sir Robert Peel, informed him that his appointment was the Queen's personal wish, he accepted. 'You shall have nothing required of you', Peel assured him.

But the centre of Wordsworth's existence remained Rydal Mount, and here his final years were weighed down by anxiety and grief. Dora, Wordsworth's surviving daughter, was especially beloved. Hartley Coleridge had noticed how 'by the mere strength of affection she entered into the recesses of her father's mind and drew him out to gambol with her in the childishness that always hung upon her womanhood'. But Hartley saw that it was an intense, and somewhat possessive love: 'strong indeed must be the love that could induce her to leave her father, whom she almost adores, and who quite doats upon her'. When, in 1838, Dora became engaged to Edward Quillinan, Wordsworth initially opposed the union – he considered a widower with an existing family and little prospects an unsuitable husband for his only daughter. He eventually gave his consent, and Dora and Quillinan were married in 1841, but tellingly, he was unable to attend the wedding, and Dora was given away by her brother William.

Dorothy, by this time, was a pale shadow of her former self. A serious illness in 1829 had left her in extreme pain. Further attacks, in 1831, 1833 and 1834 had broken her mental health. Now, the vivacious young woman of Dove Cottage, whose animated features De Quincey had so memorably described, had been reduced to a demented old woman who spent her days hunched over the fire in her room. Alcohol and opium were the only things that could relieve the constant pain, and Mary noticed how her strange behaviour 'would terrify strangers to death'. In fine weather, Wordsworth would wheel his 'dear ruin of a sister' round the garden at Rydal Mount.

As he worried about his family, the elderly poet watched old friends pass away one by one. In 1834 he lost two particularly dear friends, Coleridge in July, and in December, Charles Lamb. Coleridge, Wordsworth said, was the most wonderful man he had ever known. A year later the Scottish writer James Hogg died, and his death inspired Wordsworth to write one of his finest elegies, 'Extempore Effusion Upon the Death of James Hogg'. In the poem he remembers his departed friends.

In July 1847 came the saddest death of all. Dora's health had been weak for some time, and in May 1845 she and Quillinan visited Portugal, where she seemed to benefit from the milder climate. They returned and settled in a house close to Rydal Mount, and in October the following year Wordsworth was describing his daughter to Isabella Fenwick as being 'wonderfully strong and well'. But that Christmas Dora caught a cold, and in the spring became dangerously ill. She was moved to Rydal Mount, and by May it was clear to everyone that she was dying. 'The voice is gone', Mary Wordsworth wrote to a friend on 7 May, 'the cough and perspirations encreased—but happily her suffering from the cough is not so tearing as it had been. Her mind is clear—and her heavenward aspirations are, I doubt not, tho' in silence, her support.' Five days later, at a quarter to one in the morning, Dora died. Wordsworth informed friends of her death in expressions of Christian stoicism, and appeared to

Dora Wordsworth by Margaret Gillies, 1839.

be bearing up well to the tragedy. He devoted himself to caring for Dorothy. Privately, however, he was grief-stricken. He went for walks every day, and afterwards, Mary Wordsworth said, 'he would retire to his room sit alone & cry incessantly'. 'She is ever with me', Wordsworth wrote to Isabella Fenwick in December, 'and will be so to the last moment of my life'.

For the next two years Wordsworth waited for that last moment to come. In January 1849 Hartley Coleridge died. The day before the funeral Wordsworth and Hartley's sister Sara walked over to Grasmere churchyard, where Dora had been laid to rest, and, years earlier, little Catherine and Thomas. There Hartley was now to be buried – 'Let him lie by us', he told Sara, 'he would have wished it'. Then he asked the sexton to measure out the ground for his and Mary's own graves – 'Keep the ground for us', he said to the sexton, 'we are old people, and it cannot be long'.

The following March, Wordsworth took another walk to Grasmere. It was a cold evening, and two days later he fell ill with pleurisy. On 7 April he celebrated his eightieth birthday. Sixteen days later, on 23 April 1850, he died, as the cuckoo clock was striking the hour for noon.

A NOTE ON THIS SELECTION

The majority of the poems in this selection have been taken from three major collections which Wordsworth published in just under a decade: the first edition of *Lyrical Ballads*, published anonymously in 1798, and also containing several poems by Coleridge; the second edition of *Lyrical Ballads*, published in 1800 with an additional second volume entirely made up of new poems by Wordsworth; and *Poems, in Two Volumes*, published in 1807. Although Wordsworth revised most of these poems continually over the years, they are reproduced here in their original published form, with obvious printer's errors corrected, and two modernisations: double quotes have been changed to single quotes, and contracted words such as 'bless'd' and 'fix'd' have been expanded to 'blessed' and 'fixed'. The selection concludes with a number of Wordsworth's later poems, published between 1815 and 1842.

In addition to his published work, on his death Wordsworth left behind a huge body of unpublished manuscripts, most of which are now preserved by the Wordsworth Trust in Grasmere. This selection includes two of these manuscript poems: a transcription of 'The Ruined Cottage' made by Dorothy Wordsworth in 1799 (known as 'Manuscript D'), and a transcription dating from 1798–9, also by Dorothy, of 'The Two-Part Prelude' (known as 'Manuscript V'). Like many of Wordsworth's manuscripts, they are erratically punctuated and contain layers of later erasures and revisions. They have been printed here, as nearly as possible, in their original state, with some additional punctuation and the modernisations described above.

FROM

LYRICAL BALLADS

(1798)

LYRICAL BALLADS,

WITH

A FEW OTHER POEMS.

BRISTOL:

PRINTED BY BIGGS AND COTTLE,

FOR T. N. LONGMAN, PATERNOSTER-ROW, LONDON.

1798.

GOODY BLAKE, AND HARRY GILL,

A True Story.

Oh! what's the matter? what's the matter?
What is't that ails young Harry Gill?
That evermore his teeth they chatter,
Chatter, chatter, chatter still.
Of waistcoats Harry has no lack,
Good duffle grey, and flannel fine;
He has a blanket on his back,
And coats enough to smother nine.

In March, December, and in July,
'Tis all the same with Harry Gill;
The neighbours tell, and tell you truly,
His teeth they chatter, chatter still.
At night, at morning, and at noon,
'Tis all the same with Harry Gill;
Beneath the sun, beneath the moon,
His teeth they chatter, chatter still.

Young Harry was a lusty drover,
And who so stout of limb as he?
His cheeks were red as ruddy clover,
His voice was like the voice of three.
Auld Goody Blake was old and poor,
Ill fed she was, and thinly clad;
And any man who passed her door,
Might see how poor a hut she had.

All day she spun in her poor dwelling,
And then her three hours' work at night!
Alas! 'twas hardly worth the telling,
It would not pay for candle-light.
—This woman dwelt in Dorsetshire,
Her hut was on a cold hill-side,
And in that country coals are dear,
For they come far by wind and tide.

By the same fire to boil their pottage,
Two poor old dames, as I have known,
Will often live in one small cottage,
But she, poor woman, dwelt alone.
'Twas well enough when summer came,
The long, warm, lightsome summer-day,
Then at her door the *canty* dame
Would sit, as any linnet gay.

But when the ice our streams did fetter,
Oh! then how her old bones would shake!
You would have said, if you had met her,
'Twas a hard time for Goody Blake.
Her evenings then were dull and dead;
Sad case it was, as you may think,
For very cold to go to bed,
And then for cold not sleep a wink.

Oh joy for her! when e'er in winter
The winds at night had made a rout,
And scattered many a lusty splinter,
And many a rotten bough about.
Yet never had she, well or sick,
As every man who knew her says,
A pile before-hand, wood or stick,
Enough to warm her for three days.

Now, when the frost was past enduring,
And made her poor old bones to ache,
Could any thing be more alluring,
Than an old hedge to Goody Blake?
And now and then, it must be said,
When her old bones were cold and chill,
She left her fire, or left her bed,
To seek the hedge of Harry Gill.

Now Harry he had long suspected
This trespass of old Goody Blake,
And vowed that she should be detected,
And he on her would vengeance take.
And oft from his warm fire he'd go,
And to the fields his road would take,
And there, at night, in frost and snow,
He watched to seize old Goody Blake.

And once, behind a rick of barley,
Thus looking out did Harry stand;
The moon was full and shining clearly,
And crisp with frost the stubble-land.
—He hears a noise—he's all awake—
Again?—on tip-toe down the hill
He softly creeps—'Tis Goody Blake,
She's at the hedge of Harry Gill.

Right glad was he when he beheld her:
Stick after stick did Goody pull,
He stood behind a bush of elder,
Till she had filled her apron full.
When with her load she turned about,
The bye-road back again to take,
He started forward with a shout,
And sprang upon poor Goody Blake.

And fiercely by the arm he took her,
And by the arm he held her fast,
And fiercely by the arm he shook her,
And cried, 'I've caught you then at last!'
Then Goody, who had nothing said,
Her bundle from her lap let fall;
And kneeling on the sticks, she prayed
To God that is the judge of all.

She prayed, her withered hand uprearing,
While Harry held her by the arm—
'God! who art never out of hearing,
'O may he never more be warm!'
The cold, cold moon above her head,
Thus on her knees did Goody pray,
Young Harry heard what she had said,
And icy-cold he turned away.

He went complaining all the morrow
That he was cold and very chill:
His face was gloom, his heart was sorrow,
Alas! that day for Harry Gill!
That day he wore a riding-coat,
But not a whit the warmer he:
Another was on Thursday brought,
And ere the Sabbath he had three.

'Twas all in vain, a useless matter,
And blankets were about him pinned;
Yet still his jaws and teeth they clatter,
Like a loose casement in the wind.
And Harry's flesh it fell away;
And all who see him say 'tis plain,
That, live as long as live he may,
He never will be warm again.

No word to any man he utters,
A-bed or up, to young or old;
But ever to himself he mutters,
'Poor Harry Gill is very cold.'
A-bed or up, by night or day;
His teeth they chatter, chatter still.
Now think, ye farmers all, I pray,
Of Goody Blake and Harry Gill.

LINES

*written at a small distance from my House, and sent by
my little boy to the person to whom they are addressed.*

It is the first mild day of March:
Each minute sweeter than before,
The red-breast sings from the tall larch
That stands beside our door.

There is a blessing in the air,
Which seems a sense of joy to yield
To the bare trees, and mountains bare,
And grass in the green field.

My Sister! ('tis a wish of mine)
Now that our morning meal is done,
Make haste, your morning task resign;
Come forth and feel the sun.

Edward will come with you, and pray,
Put on with speed your woodland dress,
And bring no book, for this one day
We'll give to idleness.

No joyless forms shall regulate
Our living Calendar:
We from to-day, my friend, will date
The opening of the year.

Love, now an universal birth,
From heart to heart is stealing,
From earth to man, from man to earth,
—It is the hour of feeling.

One moment now may give us more
Than fifty years of reason;
Our minds shall drink at every pore
The spirit of the season.

Some silent laws our hearts may make,
Which they shall long obey;
We for the year to come may take
Our temper from to-day.

And from the blessed power that rolls
About, below, above;
We'll frame the measure of our souls,
They shall be tuned to love.

Then come, my sister! come, I pray,
With speed put on your woodland dress,
And bring no book; for this one day
We'll give to idleness.

WE ARE SEVEN

A simple child, dear brother Jim,
That lightly draws its breath,
And feels its life in every limb,
What should it know of death?

I met a little cottage girl,
She was eight years old, she said;
Her hair was thick with many a curl
That clustered round her head.

She had a rustic, woodland air,
And she was wildly clad;
Her eyes were fair, and very fair,
—Her beauty made me glad.

'Sisters and brothers, little maid,
'How many may you be?'
'How many? seven in all,' she said,
And wondering looked at me.

'And where are they, I pray you tell?'
She answered, 'Seven are we,
'And two of us at Conway dwell,
'And two are gone to sea.

'Two of us in the church-yard lie,
'My sister and my brother,
'And in the church-yard cottage, I
'Dwell near them with my mother.'

'You say that two at Conway dwell,
'And two are gone to sea,
'Yet you are seven; I pray you tell
'Sweet Maid, how this may be?'

Then did the little Maid reply,
'Seven boys and girls are we;
'Two of us in the church-yard lie,
'Beneath the church-yard tree.'

'You run about, my little maid,
'Your limbs they are alive;
'If two are in the church-yard laid,
'Then ye are only five.'

'Their graves are green, they may be seen,'
The little Maid replied,
'Twelve steps or more from my mother's door,
'And they are side by side.

'My stockings there I often knit,
'My 'kerchief there I hem;
'And there upon the ground I sit—
'I sit and sing to them.

'And often after sunset, Sir,
'When it is light and fair,
'I take my little porringer,
'And eat my supper there.

'The first that died was little Jane;
'In bed she moaning lay,
'Till God released her of her pain,
'And then she went away.

'So in the church-yard she was laid,
'And all the summer dry,
'Together round her grave we played,
'My brother John and I.

'And when the ground was white with snow,
'And I could run and slide,
'My brother John was forced to go,
'And he lies by her side.'

'How many are you then,' said I,
'If they two are in Heaven?'
The little Maiden did reply,
'O Master! we are seven.'

'But they are dead; those two are dead!
'Their spirits are in heaven!'
'Twas throwing words away; for still
The little Maid would have her will,
And said, 'Nay, we are seven!'

LINES

written in early Spring.

I heard a thousand blended notes,
While in a grove I sate reclined,
In that sweet mood when pleasant thoughts
Bring sad thoughts to the mind.

To her fair works did nature link
The human soul that through me ran;
And much it grieved my heart to think
What man has made of man.

Through primrose-tufts, in that sweet bower,
The periwinkle trailed its wreathes;
And 'tis my faith that every flower
Enjoys the air it breathes.

The birds around me hopped and played:
Their thoughts I cannot measure,
But the least motion which they made,
It seemed a thrill of pleasure.

The budding twigs spread out their fan,
To catch the breezy air;
And I must think, do all I can,
That there was pleasure there.

If I these thoughts may not prevent,
If such be of my creed the plan,
Have I not reason to lament
What man has made of man?

THE IDIOT BOY

'Tis eight o'clock,—a clear March night,
The moon is up—the sky is blue,
The owlet in the moonlight air,
He shouts from nobody knows where;
He lengthens out his lonely shout,
Halloo! halloo! a long halloo!

—Why bustle thus about your door,
What means this bustle, Betty Foy?
Why are you in this mighty fret?
And why on horseback have you set
Him whom you love, your idiot boy?

Beneath the moon that shines so bright,
Till she is tired, let Betty Foy
With girt and stirrup fiddle-faddle;
But wherefore set upon a saddle
Him whom she loves, her idiot boy?

There's scarce a soul that's out of bed;
Good Betty! put him down again;
His lips with joy they burr at you,
But, Betty! what has he to do
With stirrup, saddle, or with rein?

The world will say 'tis very idle,
Bethink you of the time of night;
There's not a mother, no not one,
But when she hears what you have done,
Oh! Betty she'll be in a fright.

But Betty's bent on her intent,
For her good neighbour, Susan Gale,
Old Susan, she who dwells alone,
Is sick, and makes a piteous moan,
As if her very life would fail.

There's not a house within a mile,
No hand to help them in distress:
Old Susan lies a bed in pain,
And sorely puzzled are the twain,
For what she ails they cannot guess.

And Betty's husband's at the wood,
Where by the week he doth abide,
A woodman in the distant vale;
There's none to help poor Susan Gale,
What must be done? what will betide?

And Betty from the lane has fetched
Her pony, that is mild and good,
Whether he be in joy or pain,
Feeding at will along the lane,
Or bringing faggots from the wood.

And he is all in travelling trim,
And by the moonlight, Betty Foy
Has up upon the saddle set,
The like was never heard of yet,
Him whom she loves, her idiot boy.

And he must post without delay
Across the bridge that's in the dale,
And by the church, and o'er the down,
To bring a doctor from the town,
Or she will die, old Susan Gale.

There is no need of boot or spur,
There is no need of whip or wand,
For Johnny has his holly-bough,
And with a hurly-burly now
He shakes the green bough in his hand.

And Betty o'er and o'er has told
The boy who is her best delight,
Both what to follow, what to shun,
What do, and what to leave undone,
How turn to left, and how to right.

And Betty's most especial charge,
Was, 'Johnny! Johnny! mind that you
'Come home again, nor stop at all,
'Come home again, whate'er befal,
'My Johnny do, I pray you do.'

To this did Johnny answer make,
Both with his head, and with his hand,
And proudly shook the bridle too,
And then! his words were not a few,
Which Betty well could understand.

And now that Johnny is just going,
Though Betty's in a mighty flurry,
She gently pats the pony's side,
On which her idiot boy must ride,
And seems no longer in a hurry.

But when the pony moved his legs,
Oh! then for the poor idiot boy!
For joy he cannot hold the bridle,
For joy his head and heels are idle,
He's idle all for very joy.

And while the pony moves his legs,
In Johnny's left-hand you may see,
The green bough's motionless and dead;
The moon that shines above his head
Is not more still and mute than he.

His heart it was so full of glee,
That till full fifty yards were gone,
He quite forgot his holly whip,
And all his skill in horsemanship,
Oh! happy, happy, happy John.

And Betty's standing at the door,
And Betty's face with joy o'erflows,
Proud of herself, and proud of him,
She sees him in his travelling trim;
How quietly her Johnny goes.

The silence of her idiot boy,
What hopes it sends to Betty's heart!
He's at the guide-post—he turns right,
She watches till he's out of sight,
And Betty will not then depart.

Burr, burr—now Johnny's lips they burr,
As loud as any mill, or near it,
Meek as a lamb the pony moves,
And Johnny makes the noise he loves,
And Betty listens, glad to hear it.

Away she hies to Susan Gale:
And Johnny's in a merry tune,
The owlets hoot, the owlets curr,
And Johnny's lips they burr, burr, burr,
And on he goes beneath the moon.

His steed and he right well agree,
For of this pony there's a rumour,
That should he lose his eyes and ears,
And should he live a thousand years,
He never will be out of humour.

But then he is a horse that thinks!
And when he thinks his pace is slack;
Now, though he knows poor Johnny well,
Yet for his life he cannot tell
What he has got upon his back.

So through the moonlight lanes they go,
And far into the moonlight dale,
And by the church, and o'er the down,
To bring a doctor from the town,
To comfort poor old Susan Gale.

And Betty, now at Susan's side,
Is in the middle of her story,
What comfort Johnny soon will bring,
With many a most diverting thing,
Of Johnny's wit and Johnny's glory.

And Betty's still at Susan's side:
By this time she's not quite so flurried;
Demure with porringer and plate
She sits, as if in Susan's fate
Her life and soul were buried.

But Betty, poor good woman! she,
You plainly in her face may read it,
Could lend out of that moment's store
Five years of happiness or more,
To any that might need it.

But yet I guess that now and then
With Betty all was not so well,
And to the road she turns her ears,
And thence full many a sound she hears,
Which she to Susan will not tell.

Poor Susan moans, poor Susan groans,
'As sure as there's a moon in heaven,'
Cries Betty, 'he'll be back again;
'They'll both be here, 'tis almost ten,
'They'll both be here before eleven.'

Poor Susan moans, poor Susan groans,
The clock gives warning for eleven;
'Tis on the stroke—'If Johnny's near,'
Quoth Betty 'he will soon be here,
'As sure as there's a moon in heaven.'

The clock is on the stroke of twelve,
And Johnny is not yet in sight,
The moon's in heaven, as Betty sees,
But Betty is not quite at ease;
And Susan has a dreadful night.

And Betty, half an hour ago,
On Johnny vile reflections cast;
'A little idle sauntering thing!'
With other names, an endless string,
But now that time is gone and past.

And Betty's drooping at the heart,
That happy time all past and gone,
'How can it be he is so late?
'The doctor he has made him wait,
'Susan! they'll both be here anon.'

And Susan's growing worse and worse,
And Betty's in a sad quandary;
And then there's nobody to say
If she must go or she must stay:
—She's in a sad quandary.

The clock is on the stroke of one;
But neither Doctor nor his guide
Appear along the moonlight road,
There's neither horse nor man abroad,
And Betty's still at Susan's side.

And Susan she begins to fear
Of sad mischances not a few,
That Johnny may perhaps be drowned,
Or lost perhaps, and never found;
Which they must both for ever rue.

She prefaced half a hint of this
With, 'God forbid it should be true!'
At the first word that Susan said
Cried Betty, rising from the bed,
'Susan, I'd gladly stay with you.

'I must be gone, I must away,
'Consider, Johnny's but half-wise;
'Susan, we must take care of him,
'If he is hurt in life or limb'—
'Oh God forbid!' poor Susan cries.

'What can I do?' says Betty, going,
'What can I do to ease your pain?
'Good Susan tell me, and I'll stay;
'I fear you're in a dreadful way,
'But I shall soon be back again.'

'Good Betty go, good Betty go,
'There's nothing that can ease my pain.'
Then off she hies, but with a prayer
That God poor Susan's life would spare,
Till she comes back again.

So, through the moonlight lane she goes,
And far into the moonlight dale;
And how she ran, and how she walked,
And all that to herself she talked,
Would surely be a tedious tale.

In high and low, above, below,
In great and small, in round and square,
In tree and tower was Johnny seen,
In bush and brake, in black and green,
'Twas Johnny, Johnny, every where.

She's past the bridge that's in the dale,
And now the thought torments her sore,
Johnny perhaps his horse forsook,
To hunt the moon that's in the brook,
And never will be heard of more.

And now she's high upon the down,
Alone amid a prospect wide;
There's neither Johnny nor his horse,
Among the fern or in the gorse;
There's neither doctor nor his guide.

'Oh saints! what is become of him?
'Perhaps he's climbed into an oak,
'Where he will stay till he is dead;
'Or sadly he has been misled,
'And joined the wandering gypsey-folk.

'Or him that wicked pony's carried
'To the dark cave, the goblins' hall,
'Or in the castle he's pursuing,
'Among the ghosts, his own undoing;
'Or playing with the waterfall.'

At poor old Susan then she railed,
While to the town she posts away;
'If Susan had not been so ill,
'Alas! I should have had him still,
'My Johnny, till my dying day.'

Poor Betty! in this sad distemper,
The doctor's self would hardly spare,
Unworthy things she talked and wild,
Even he, of cattle the most mild,
The pony had his share.

And now she's got into the town,
And to the doctor's door she hies;
'Tis silence all on every side;
The town so long, the town so wide,
Is silent as the skies.

And now she's at the doctor's door,
She lifts the knocker, rap, rap, rap,
The doctor at the casement shews,
His glimmering eyes that peep and doze;
And one hand rubs his old night-cap.

'Oh Doctor! Doctor! where's my Johnny?'
'I'm here, what is't you want with me?'
'Oh Sir! you know I'm Betty Foy,
'And I have lost my poor dear boy,
'You know him—him you often see;

'He's not so wise as some folks be,'
'The devil take his wisdom!' said
The Doctor, looking somewhat grim,
'What, woman! should I know of him?'
And, grumbling, he went back to bed.

'O woe is me! O woe is me!
'Here will I die; here will I die;
'I thought to find my Johnny here,
'But he is neither far nor near,
'Oh! what a wretched mother I!'

She stops, she stands, she looks about,
Which way to turn she cannot tell.
Poor Betty! it would ease her pain
If she had heart to knock again;
—The clock strikes three—a dismal knell!

Then up along the town she hies,
No wonder if her senses fail,
This piteous news so much it shocked her,
She quite forgot to send the Doctor,
To comfort poor old Susan Gale.

And now she's high upon the down,
And she can see a mile of road,
'Oh cruel! I'm almost three-score;
'Such night as this was ne'er before,
'There's not a single soul abroad.'

She listens, but she cannot hear
The foot of horse, the voice of man;
The streams with softest sound are flowing,
The grass you almost hear it growing,
You hear it now if e'er you can.

The owlets through the long blue night
Are shouting to each other still:
Fond lovers, yet not quite hob nob,
They lengthen out the tremulous sob,
That echoes far from hill to hill.

Poor Betty now has lost all hope,
Her thoughts are bent on deadly sin;
A green-grown pond she just has passed,
And from the brink she hurries fast,
Lest she should drown herself therein.

And now she sits her down and weeps;
Such tears she never shed before;
'Oh dear, dear pony! my sweet joy!
'Oh carry back my idiot boy!
'And we will ne'er o'erload thee more.'

A thought is come into her head;
'The pony he is mild and good,
'And we have always used him well;
'Perhaps he's gone along the dell,
'And carried Johnny to the wood.'

Then up she springs as if on wings;
She thinks no more of deadly sin;
If Betty fifty ponds should see,
The last of all her thoughts would be,
To drown herself therein.

Oh reader! now that I might tell
What Johnny and his horse are doing!
What they've been doing all this time,
Oh could I put it into rhyme,
A most delightful tale pursuing!

Perhaps, and no unlikely thought!
He with his pony now doth roam
The cliffs and peaks so high that are,
To lay his hands upon a star,
And in his pocket bring it home.

Perhaps he's turned himself about,
His face unto his horse's tail,
And still and mute, in wonder lost,
All like a silent horseman-ghost,
He travels on along the vale.

And now, perhaps, he's hunting sheep,
A fierce and dreadful hunter he!
Yon valley, that's so trim and green,
In five months' time, should he be seen,
A desart wilderness will be.

Perhaps, with head and heels on fire,
And like the very soul of evil,
He's galloping away, away,
And so he'll gallop on for aye,
The bane of all that dread the devil.

I to the muses have been bound,
These fourteen years, by strong indentures;
Oh gentle muses! let me tell
But half of what to him befel,
For sure he met with strange adventures.

Oh gentle muses! is this kind?
Why will ye thus my suit repel?
Why of your further aid bereave me?
And can you thus unfriended leave me?
Ye muses! whom I love so well.

Who's yon, that, near the waterfall,
Which thunders down with headlong force,
Beneath the moon, yet shining fair,
As careless as if nothing were,
Sits upright on a feeding horse?

Unto his horse, that's feeding free,
He seems, I think, the rein to give;
Of moon or stars he takes no heed;
Of such we in romances read,
— 'Tis Johnny! Johnny! as I live.

And that's the very pony too.
Where is she, where is Betty Foy?
She hardly can sustain her fears;
The roaring water-fall she hears,
And cannot find her idiot boy.

Your pony's worth his weight in gold,
Then calm your terrors, Betty Foy!
She's coming from among the trees,
And now, all full in view, she sees
Him whom she loves, her idiot boy.

And Betty sees the pony too:
Why stand you thus Good Betty Foy?
It is no goblin, 'tis no ghost,
'Tis he whom you so long have lost,
He whom you love, your idiot boy.

She looks again—her arms are up—
She screams—she cannot move for joy;
She darts as with a torrent's force,
She almost has o'erturned the horse,
And fast she holds her idiot boy.

And Johnny burrs and laughs aloud,
Whether in cunning or in joy,
I cannot tell; but while he laughs,
Betty a drunken pleasure quaffs,
To hear again her idiot boy.

And now she's at the pony's tail,
And now she's at the pony's head,
On that side now, and now on this,
And almost stifled with her bliss,
A few sad tears does Betty shed.

She kisses o'er and o'er again,
Him whom she loves, her idiot boy,
She's happy here, she's happy there,
She is uneasy every where:
Her limbs are all alive with joy.

She pats the pony, where or when
She knows not, happy Betty Foy!
The little pony glad may be,
But he is milder far than she,
You hardly can perceive his joy.

'Oh! Johnny, never mind the Doctor;
'You've done your best, and that is all.'
She took the reins, when this was said,
And gently turned the pony's head
From the loud water-fall.

By this the stars were almost gone,
The moon was setting on the hill,
So pale you scarcely looked at her:
The little birds began to stir,
Though yet their tongues were still.

The pony, Betty, and her boy,
Wind slowly through the woody dale:
And who is she, be-times abroad,
That hobbles up the steep rough road?
Who is it, but old Susan Gale?

Long Susan lay deep lost in thought,
And many dreadful fears beset her,
Both for her messenger and nurse;
And as her mind grew worse and worse,
Her body it grew better.

She turned, she tossed herself in bed,
On all sides doubts and terrors met her;
Point after point did she discuss;
And while her mind was fighting thus,
Her body still grew better.

'Alas! what is become of them?
'These fears can never be endured,
'I'll to the wood.'—The word scarce said,
Did Susan rise up from her bed,
As if by magic cured.

Away she posts up hill and down,
And to the wood at length is come,
She spies her friends, she shouts a greeting;
Oh me! it is a merry meeting,
As ever was in Christendom.

The owls have hardly sung their last,
While our four travellers homeward wend;
The owls have hooted all night long,
And with the owls began my song,
And with the owls must end.

For while they all were travelling home,
Cried Betty, 'Tell us Johnny, do,
'Where all this long night you have been,
'What you have heard, what you have seen,
'And Johnny, mind you tell us true.'

Now Johnny all night long had heard
The owls in tuneful concert strive;
No doubt too he the moon had seen;
For in the moonlight he had been
From eight o'clock till five.

And thus to Betty's question, he
Made answer, like a traveller bold,
(His very words I give to you,)
'The cocks did crow to-whoo, to-whoo,
'And the sun did shine so cold.'
—Thus answered Johnny in his glory,
And that was all his travel's story.

EXPOSTULATION AND REPLY

'Why, William, on that old grey stone,
'Thus for the length of half a day,
'Why, William, sit you thus alone,
'And dream your time away?

'Where are your books? that light bequeathed
'To beings else forlorn and blind!
'Up! Up! and drink the spirit breathed
'From dead men to their kind.

'You look round on your mother earth,
'As if she for no purpose bore you;
'As if you were her first-born birth,
'And none had lived before you!'

One morning thus, by Esthwaite lake,
When life was sweet I knew not why,
To me my good friend Matthew spake,
And thus I made reply.

'The eye it cannot chuse but see,
'We cannot bid the ear be still;
'Our bodies feel, where'er they be,
'Against, or with our will.

'Nor less I deem that there are powers,
'Which of themselves our minds impress,
'That we can feed this mind of ours,
'In a wise passiveness.

'Think you, mid all this mighty sum
'Of things for ever speaking,
'That nothing of itself will come,
'But we must still be seeking?

'—Then ask not wherefore, here, alone,
'Conversing as I may,
'I sit upon this old grey stone,
'And dream my time away.'

THE TABLES TURNED;
an Evening Scene, on the same Subject.

Up! up! my friend, and clear your looks,
Why all this toil and trouble?
Up! up! my friend, and quit your books,
Or surely you'll grow double.

The sun, above the mountain's head,
A freshening lustre mellow,
Through all the long green fields has spread,
His first sweet evening yellow.

Books! 'tis a dull and endless strife,
Come, hear the woodland linnet,
How sweet his music; on my life
There's more of wisdom in it.

And hark! how blithe the throstle sings!
And he is no mean preacher;
Come forth into the light of things,
Let Nature be your teacher.

She has a world of ready wealth,
Our minds and hearts to bless—
Spontaneous wisdom breathed by health,
Truth breathed by chearfulness.

One impulse from a vernal wood
May teach you more of man;
Of moral evil and of good,
Than all the sages can.

Sweet is the lore which nature brings;
Our meddling intellect
Mishapes the beauteous forms of things;
—We murder to dissect.

Enough of science and of art;
Close up these barren leaves;
Come forth, and bring with you a heart
That watches and receives.

OLD MAN TRAVELLING;

Animal Tranquillity and Decay, a Sketch.

                    The little hedge-row birds,
That peck along the road, regard him not.
He travels on, and in his face, his step,
His gait, is one expression; every limb,
His look and bending figure, all bespeak
A man who does not move with pain, but moves
With thought—He is insensibly subdued
To settled quiet: he is one by whom
All effort seems forgotten, one to whom
Long patience has such mild composure given,
That patience now doth seem a thing, of which
He hath no need. He is by nature led
To peace so perfect, that the young behold
With envy, what the old man hardly feels.
—I asked him whither he was bound, and what
The object of his journey; he replied
'Sir! I am going many miles to take
'A last leave of my son, a mariner,
'Who from a sea-fight has been brought to Falmouth,
'And there is dying in an hospital.'

LINES

*written a few miles above TINTERN ABBEY,
on revisiting the banks of the WYE during a Tour.
July 13, 1798.*

Five years have passed; five summers, with the length
Of five long winters! and again I hear
These waters, rolling from their mountain-springs
With a sweet inland murmur.*—Once again
Do I behold these steep and lofty cliffs,
Which on a wild secluded scene impress
Thoughts of more deep seclusion; and connect
The landscape with the quiet of the sky.
The day is come when I again repose
Here, under this dark sycamore, and view
These plots of cottage-ground, these orchard-tufts,
Which, at this season, with their unripe fruits,
Among the woods and copses lose themselves,
Nor, with their green and simple hue, disturb
The wild green landscape. Once again I see
These hedge-rows, hardly hedge-rows, little lines
Of sportive wood run wild; these pastoral farms
Green to the very door; and wreathes of smoke
Sent up, in silence, from among the trees,
With some uncertain notice, as might seem,
Of vagrant dwellers in the houseless woods,
Or of some hermit's cave, where by his fire
The hermit sits alone.
                              Though absent long,
These forms of beauty have not been to me,

*The river is not affected by the tides a few miles above Tintern.

As is a landscape to a blind man's eye:
But oft, in lonely rooms, and mid the din
Of towns and cities, I have owed to them,
In hours of weariness, sensations sweet,
Felt in the blood, and felt along the heart,
And passing even into my purer mind
With tranquil restoration:—feelings too
Of unremembered pleasure; such, perhaps,
As may have had no trivial influence
On that best portion of a good man's life;
His little, nameless, unremembered acts
Of kindness and of love. Nor less, I trust,
To them I may have owed another gift,
Of aspect more sublime; that blessed mood,
In which the burthen of the mystery,
In which the heavy and the weary weight
Of all this unintelligible world
Is lightened:—that serene and blessed mood,
In which the affections gently lead us on,
Until, the breath of this corporeal frame,
And even the motion of our human blood
Almost suspended, we are laid asleep
In body, and become a living soul:
While with an eye made quiet by the power
Of harmony, and the deep power of joy,
We see into the life of things.

                                        If this
Be but a vain belief, yet, oh! how oft,
In darkness, and amid the many shapes
Of joyless day-light; when the fretful stir
Unprofitable, and the fever of the world,
Have hung upon the beatings of my heart,

How oft, in spirit, have I turned to thee
O sylvan Wye! Thou wanderer through the woods,
How often has my spirit turned to thee!

And now, with gleams of half-extinguished thought,
With many recognitions dim and faint,
And somewhat of a sad perplexity,
The picture of the mind revives again:
While here I stand, not only with the sense
Of present pleasure, but with pleasing thoughts
That in this moment there is life and food
For future years. And so I dare to hope
Though changed, no doubt, from what I was, when first
I came among these hills; when like a roe
I bounded o'er the mountains, by the sides
Of the deep rivers, and the lonely streams,
Wherever nature led; more like a man
Flying from something that he dreads, than one
Who sought the thing he loved. For nature then
(The coarser pleasures of my boyish days,
And their glad animal movements all gone by,)
To me was all in all.—I cannot paint
What then I was. The sounding cataract
Haunted me like a passion: the tall rock,
The mountain, and the deep and gloomy wood,
Their colours and their forms, were then to me
An appetite: a feeling and a love,
That had no need of a remoter charm,
By thought supplied, or any interest
Unborrowed from the eye.—That time is past,
And all its aching joys are now no more,
And all its dizzy raptures. Not for this

Faint I, nor mourn nor murmur: other gifts
Have followed, for such loss, I would believe,
Abundant recompence. For I have learned
To look on nature, not as in the hour
Of thoughtless youth, but hearing oftentimes
The still, sad music of humanity,
Not harsh nor grating, though of ample power
To chasten and subdue. And I have felt
A presence that disturbs me with the joy
Of elevated thoughts; a sense sublime
Of something far more deeply interfused,
Whose dwelling is the light of setting suns,
And the round ocean, and the living air,
And the blue sky, and in the mind of man,
A motion and a spirit, that impels
All thinking things, all objects of all thought,
And rolls through all things. Therefore am I still
A lover of the meadows and the woods,
And mountains; and of all that we behold
From this green earth; of all the mighty world
Of eye and ear, both what they half-create,*
And what perceive; well pleased to recognize
In nature and the language of the sense,
The anchor of my purest thoughts, the nurse,
The guide, the guardian of my heart, and soul
Of all my moral being.
                              Nor, perchance,
If I were not thus taught, should I the more
Suffer my genial spirits to decay:
For thou art with me, here, upon the banks

*This line has a close resemblance to an admirable line of
Young, the exact expression of which I cannot recollect.

Of this fair river; thou, my dearest Friend,
My dear, dear Friend, and in thy voice I catch
The language of my former heart, and read
My former pleasures in the shooting lights
Of thy wild eyes. Oh! yet a little while
May I behold in thee what I was once,
My dear, dear Sister! And this prayer I make,
Knowing that Nature never did betray
The heart that loved her; 'tis her privilege,
Through all the years of this our life, to lead
From joy to joy: for she can so inform
The mind that is within us, so impress
With quietness and beauty, and so feed
With lofty thoughts, that neither evil tongues,
Rash judgements, nor the sneers of selfish men,
Nor greetings where no kindness is, nor all
The dreary intercourse of daily life,
Shall e'er prevail against us, or disturb
Our chearful faith that all which we behold
Is full of blessings. Therefore let the moon
Shine on thee in thy solitary walk;
And let the misty mountain winds be free
To blow against thee: and in after years,
When these wild ecstasies shall be matured
Into a sober pleasure, when thy mind
Shall be a mansion for all lovely forms,
Thy memory be as a dwelling-place
For all sweet sounds and harmonies; Oh! then,
If solitude, or fear, or pain, or grief,
Should be thy portion, with what healing thoughts
Of tender joy wilt thou remember me,
And these my exhortations! Nor, perchance,

If I should be, where I no more can hear
Thy voice, nor catch from thy wild eyes these gleams
Of past existence, wilt thou then forget
That on the banks of this delightful stream
We stood together; and that I, so long
A worshipper of Nature, hither came,
Unwearied in that service: rather say
With warmer love, oh! with far deeper zeal
Of holier love. Nor wilt thou then forget,
That after many wanderings, many years
Of absence, these steep woods and lofty cliffs,
And this green pastoral landscape, were to me
More dear, both for themselves, and for thy sake.

THE RUINED COTTAGE

'Manuscript D' (1799)

(MS D)

The Ruined Cottage
1st Part

'Twas summer & the sun was mounted high
Along the south the uplands feebly glared
Through a pale steam, & all the northern downs
In clearer air ascending shewed far off
Their surfaces with shadows dappled o'er
Of deep embattled clouds: far as the sight
Could reach those many shadows lay in spots
Determined & unmoved, with steady beams
Of clear & pleasant sunshine interposed
Pleasant to him who on the soft cool moss
Extends his careless limbs along the root
Of some huge oak whose aged branches make
A twilight of their own, a dewy shade
Where the wren warbles while the dreaming man
Half-conscious of that soothing melody
With sidelong eye looks out upon the scene
By those impending branches made more soft
More soft and distant. Other lot was mine
Across a bare wide common I had toiled
With languid feet which by the slipping ground
Were baffled still, & when I stretched myself
On the brown earth my limbs from very
The host of insects where in I could be at

THE RUINED COTTAGE

1st Part

'Twas summer and the sun was mounted high.
Along the south the uplands feebly glared
Through a pale steam, and all the northern downs
In clearer air ascending shewed far off
Their surfaces with shadows dappled o'er
Of deep embattled clouds: far as the sight
Could reach those many shadows lay in spots
Determined and unmoved, with steady beams
Of clear and pleasant sunshine interposed.
Pleasant to him who on the soft cool moss
Extends his careless limbs beside the root
Of some huge oak whose aged branches make
A twilight of their own, a dewy shade
Where the wren warbles while the dreaming man,
Half-conscious of that soothing melody,
With side-long eye looks out upon the scene
By those impending branches made more soft,
More soft and distant. Other lot was mine.
Across a bare wide Common I had toiled
With languid feet which by the slipp'ry ground
Were baffled still, and when I stretched myself
On the brown earth my limbs from very heat
Could find no rest nor my weak arm disperse
The insect host which gathered round my face
And joined their murmurs to the tedious noise
Of seeds and bursting gorse that crackled round.
I rose and turned towards a group of trees
Which midway in that level stood alone,

And thither come at length beneath a shade
Of clustering elms that sprang from the same root
I found a ruined house, four naked walls
That stared upon each other. I looked round
And near the door I saw an aged Man,
Alone, and stretched upon the cottage bench;
An iron-pointed staff lay at his side.
With instantaneous joy I recognized
That pride of nature and of lowly life,
The venerable Armytage, a friend
As dear to me as is the setting sun.
                    Two days before
We had been fellow-travellers. I knew
That he was in this neighbourhood and now
Delighted found him here in the cool shade.
He lay, his pack of rustic merchandize
Pillowing his head—I guess he had no thought
Of his way-wandering life. His eyes were shut,
The shadows of the breezy elms above
Dappled his face. With thirsty heat oppress'd
At length I hailed him, glad to see his hat
Bedewed with water-drops, as if the brim
Had newly scoop'd a running stream. He rose,
And pointing to a sun-flower bade me climb
The   wall where that same gaudy flower
Looked out upon the road. It was a plot
Of garden-ground, now wild, its matted weeds
Marked with the steps of those whom as they pass'd,
The goose-berry trees that shot in long lank slips,
Or currants hanging from their leafless stems
In scanty strings, had tempted to o'erleap
The broken wall. Within that cheerless spot,

Where two tall hedgerows of thick willow boughs
Joined in a damp cold nook, I found a well
Half-choked with willow flowers and weeds.
I slaked my thirst and to the shady bench
Returned, and while I stood unbonneted
To catch the motion of the cooler air
The old Man said, 'I see around me here
Things which you cannot see, we die, my Friend,
Nor we alone, but that which each man loved
And prized in his peculiar nook of earth
Dies with him or is changed, and very soon
Even of the good is no memorial left.
The Poets in their elegies and songs
Lamenting the departed call the groves,
They call upon the hills and streams to mourn,
And senseless rocks, nor idly: for, they speak
In these their invocations with a voice
Obedient to the strong creative power
Of human passion. Sympathies there are
More tranquil, yet perhaps of kindred birth,
That steal upon the meditative mind
And grow with thought. Beside yon spring I stood
And eyed its waters till we seemed to feel
One sadness, they and I. For them a bond
Of brotherhood is broken: time has been
When every day the touch of human hand
Disturbed their stillness, and they ministered
To human comfort. When I stooped to drink,
A spider's web hung to the water's edge,
And on the wet and slimy foot-stone lay
The useless fragment of a wooden bowl;
It moved my very heart. The day has been

When I could never pass this road but she
Who lived within these walls, when I appeared
A daughter's welcome gave me, and I loved her
As my own child. O Sir! the good die first,
And they whose hearts are dry as summer dust
Burn to the socket. Many a passenger
Has blessed poor Margaret for her gentle looks
When she upheld the cool refreshment drawn
From that forsaken spring, and no one came
But he was welcome, no one went away
But that it seemed she loved him. She is dead,
The worm is on her cheek, and this poor hut,
Stripp'd of its outward garb of household flowers
Of rose and sweet-briar, offers to the wind
A cold bare wall whose earthy top is tricked
With weeds and the rank spear-grass. She is dead,
And nettles rot and adders sun themselves
Where we have sate together while she nurs'd
Her infant at her breast. The unshod Colt,
The wandring heifer, and the Potter's ass
Find shelter now within the chimney-wall
Where I have seen her evening hearth-stone blaze
And through the window spread upon the road
Its chearful light.—You will forgive me, Sir,
But often on this cottage do I muse
As on a picture, till my wiser mind
Sinks, yielding to the foolishness of grief.

    She had a husband, an industrious man,
Sober and steady. I have heard her say
That he was up and busy at his loom
In summer ere the mower's scythe had swept
The dewy grass, and in the early spring

Ere the last star had vanished. They who pass'd
At evening from behind the garden-fence
Might hear his busy spade, which he would ply
After his daily work till the day-light
Was gone and every leaf and flower were lost
In the dark hedges. So they pass'd their days
In peace and comfort, and two pretty babes
Were their best hope next to the God in Heaven.
—You may remember, now some ten years gone,
Two blighting seasons when the fields were left
With half a harvest. It pleased heaven to add
A worse affliction in the plague of war:
A happy land was stricken to the heart;
'Twas a sad time of sorrow and distress.
A wanderer among the cottages,
I with my pack of winter raiment saw
The hardships of that season: many rich
Sunk down as in a dream among the poor,
And of the poor did many cease to be,
And their place knew them not. Meanwhile, abridg'd
Of daily comforts, gladly reconciled
To numerous self-denials, Margaret
Went struggling on through those calamitous years
With chearful hope: but ere the second autumn
A fever seized her husband. In disease
He lingered long, and when his strength returned
He found the little he had stored to meet
The hour of accident or crippling age
Was all consumed. As I have said, 'twas now
A time of trouble: shoals of artisans
Were from their daily labour turned away
To hang for bread on parish charity,

They and their wives and children—happier far
Could they have lived as do the little birds
That peck along the hedges or the kite
That makes her dwelling in the mountain rocks.
Ill fared it now with Robert, he who dwelt
In this poor cottage; at his door he stood
And whistled many a snatch of merry tunes
That had no mirth in them, or with his knife
Carved uncouth figures on the heads of sticks,
Then idly sought about through every nook
Of house or garden any casual task
Of use or ornament, and with a strange,
Amusing but uneasy novelty
He blended where he might the various tasks
Of summer, autumn, winter, and of spring.
But this endured not; his good-humour soon
Became a weight in which no pleasure was,
And poverty brought on a petted mood
And a sore temper: day by day he drooped,
And he would leave his home and to the town
Without an errand would he turn his steps,
Or wander here and there among the fields.
One while he would speak lightly of his babes
And with a cruel tongue, at other times
He played with them wild freaks of merriment,
And 'twas a piteous thing to see the looks
Of the poor innocent children. 'Every smile,'
Said Margaret to me here beneath these trees,
"Made my heart bleed."' At this the old Man paus'd,
And looking up to those enormous elms
He said, ' 'Tis now the hour of deepest noon.
At this still season of repose and peace,

This hour when all things which are not at rest
Are chearful, while this multitude of flies
Fills all the air with happy melody,
Why should a tear be in an old man's eye?
Why should we thus with an untoward mind
And in the weakness of humanity
From natural wisdom turn our hearts away,
To natural comfort shut our eyes and ears,
And feeding on disquiet thus disturb
The calm of Nature with our restless thoughts?'

End of the first Part

He spake with somewhat of a solemn tone,
But when he ended there was in his face
Such easy chearfulness, a look so mild
That for a little time it stole away
All recollection, and that simple tale
Passed from my mind like a forgotten sound.
A while on trivial things we held discourse,
To me soon tasteless. In my own despite
I thought of that poor woman as of one
Whom I had known and loved. He had rehearsed
Her homely tale with such familiar power,
With such an active countenance, an eye
So busy, that the things of which he spake
Seemed present, and, attention now relaxed,
There was a heartfelt chillness in my veins.
I rose, and turning from that breezy shade
Went out into the open air and stood
To drink the comfort of the warmer sun.
Long time I had not stayed ere, looking round
Upon that tranquil ruin, I returned
And begged of the old man that for my sake
He would resume his story. He replied,
'It were a wantonness and would demand
Severe reproof, if we were men whose hearts
Could hold vain dalliance with the misery
Even of the dead, contented thence to draw
A momentary pleasure never marked
By reason, barren of all future good.
But we have known that there is often found
In mournful thoughts, and always might be found,

A power to virtue friendly; were't not so,
I am a dreamer among men, indeed
An idle dreamer. 'Tis a common tale,
By moving accidents uncharactered,
A tale of silent suffering, hardly clothed
In bodily form, and to the grosser sense
But ill adapted, scarcely palpable
To him who does not think. But at your bidding
I will proceed.

              While thus it fared with them
To whom this cottage till that hapless year
Had been a blessed home, it was my chance
To travel in a country far remote.
And glad I was when, halting by yon gate
That leads from the green lane, again I saw
Those lofty elm-trees. Long I did not rest:
With many pleasant thoughts I cheer'd my way
O'er the flat common. At the door arrived,
I knocked, and when I entered with the hope
Of usual greeting, Margaret looked at me
A little while, then turned her head away
Speechless, and sitting down upon a chair
Wept bitterly. I wist not what to do
Or how to speak to her. Poor wretch! at last
She rose from off her seat—and then, oh Sir!
I cannot tell how she pronounced my name:
With fervent love, and with a face of grief
Unutterably helpless, and a look
That seem'd to cling upon me, she enquir'd
If I had seen her husband. As she spake
A strange surprize and fear came to my heart,
Nor had I power to answer ere she told

That he had disappeared; just two months gone.
He left his house; two wretched days had passed,
And on the third by the first break of light
Within her casement full in view she saw
A purse of gold. 'I trembled at the sight,'
Said Margaret, 'for I knew it was his hand
That placed it there, and on that very day
By one, a stranger, from my husband sent,
The tidings came that he had joined a troop
Of soldiers going to a distant land.
He left me thus—Poor Man! he had not heart
To take a farewell of me, and he feared
That I should follow with my babes, and sink
Beneath the misery of a soldier's life.'
This tale did Margaret tell with many tears,
And when she ended I had little power
To give her comfort, and was glad to take
Such words of hope from her own mouth as serv'd
To cheer us both; but long we had not talked
Ere we built up a pile of better thoughts,
And with a brighter eye she looked around
As if she had been shedding tears of joy.
We parted. It was then the early spring;
I left her busy with her garden tools,
And well remember, o'er that fence she looked,
And while I paced along the foot-way path
Called out, and sent a blessing after me
With tender chearfulness and with a voice
That seemed the very sound of happy thoughts.

    I roved o'er many a hill and many a dale
With this my weary load, in heat and cold,
Through many a wood, and many an open ground,

In sunshine or in shade, in wet or fair,
Now blithe, now drooping, as it might befal,
My best companions now the driving winds
And now the 'trotting brooks' and whispering trees
And now the music of my own sad steps,
With many a short-lived thought that pass'd between
And disappeared. I came this way again
Towards the wane of summer, when the wheat
Was yellow, and the soft and bladed grass
Sprang up afresh and o'er the hay-field spread
Its tender green. When I had reached the door
I found that she was absent. In her shade
Where now we sit I waited her return.
Her cottage in its outward look appeared
As chearful as before; in any shew
Of neatness little changed, but that I thought
The honeysuckle crowded round the door
And from the wall hung down in heavier wreathes,
And knots of worthless stone-crop started out
Along the window's edge, and grew like weeds
Against the lower panes. I turned aside
And stroll'd into her garden.—It was changed:
The unprofitable bindweed spread his bells
From side to side and with unwieldy wreaths
Had dragged the rose from its sustaining wall
And bent it down to earth; the border-tufts,
Daisy and thrift and lowly camomile
And thyme, had straggled out into the paths
Which they were used to deck. Ere this an hour
Was wasted. Back I turned my restless steps,
And as I walked before the door it chanced
A stranger passed, and guessing whom I sought

He said that she was used to ramble far.
The sun was sinking in the west, and now
I sate with sad impatience. From within
Her solitary infant cried aloud.
The spot though fair seemed very desolate,
The longer I remained more desolate.
And, looking round, I saw the corner-stones,
Till then unmark'd, on either side the door
With dull red stains discoloured and stuck o'er
With tufts and hairs of wool, as if the sheep
That feed upon the commons thither came
Familiarly and found a couching-place
Even at her threshold.—The house-clock struck eight;
I turned and saw her distant a few steps.
Her face was pale and thin, her figure too
Was chang'd. As she unlocked the door she said,
'It grieves me you have waited here so long,
But in good truth I've wandered much of late
And sometimes, to my shame I speak, have need
Of my best prayers to bring me back again.'
While on the board she spread our evening meal
She told me she had lost her elder child,
That he for months had been a serving-boy
Apprenticed by the parish. 'I perceive
You look at me, and you have cause. Today
I have been travelling far, and many days
About the fields I wander, knowing this
Only, that what I seek I cannot find.
And so I waste my time, for I am changed,
And to myself,' said she, 'have done much wrong,
And to this helpless infant. I have slept
Weeping, and weeping I have waked; my tears

Have flow'd as if my body were not such
As others are, and I could never die.
But I am now in mind and in my heart
More easy, and I hope,' said she, 'that heaven
Will give me patience to endure the things
Which I behold at home.' It would have grieved
Your very heart to see her. Sir, I feel
The story linger in my heart. I fear
'Tis long and tedious, but my spirit clings
To that poor woman: so familiarly
Do I perceive her manner, and her look
And presence, and so deeply do I feel
Her goodness, that not seldom in my walks
A momentary trance comes over me,
And to myself I seem to muse on one
By sorrow laid asleep or borne away,
A human being destined to awake
To human life, or something very near
To human life, when he shall come again
For whom she suffered. Sir, it would have griev'd
Your very soul to see her: evermore
Her eye-lids droop'd, her eyes were downward cast,
And when she at her table gave me food
She did not look at me. Her voice was low,
Her body was subdued. In every act
Pertaining to her house-affairs appeared
The careless stillness which a thinking mind
Gives to an idle matter—still she sighed,
But yet no motion of the breast was seen,
No heaving of the heart. While by the fire
We sate together, sighs came on my ear;
I knew not how, and hardly whence they came.

I took my staff, and when I kissed her babe
The tears stood in her eyes. I left her then
With the best hope and comfort I could give;
She thanked me for my will, but for my hope
It seemed she did not thank me.
                                          I returned
And took my rounds along this road again
Ere on its sunny bank the primrose flower
Had chronicled the earliest day of spring.
I found her sad and drooping; she had learn'd
No tidings of her husband: if he lived
She knew not that he lived; if he were dead
She knew not he was dead. She seemed the same
In person or appearance, but her house
Bespoke a sleepy hand of negligence:
The floor was neither dry nor neat, the hearth
Was comfortless   ,
The windows too were dim, and her few books,
Which, one upon the other, heretofore
Had been piled up against the corner-panes
In seemly order, now with straggling leaves
Lay scattered here and there, open or shut
As they had chanced to fall. Her infant babe
Had from its mother caught the trick of grief
And sighed among its playthings. Once again
I turned towards the garden-gate and saw
More plainly still that poverty and grief
Were now come nearer to her: the earth was hard,
With weeds defaced and knots of withered grass;
No ridges there appeared of clear black mould,
No winter greenness; of her herbs and flowers
It seemed the better part were gnawed away

Or trampled on the earth; a chain of straw
Which had been twisted round the tender stem
Of a young apple-tree lay at its root;
The bark was nibbled round by truant sheep.
Margaret stood near, her infant in her arms,
And seeing that my eye was on the tree
She said, 'I fear it will be dead and gone
Ere Robert come again.' Towards the house
Together we returned, and she inquired
If I had any hope. But for her Babe
And for her little friendless Boy, she said,
She had no wish to live, that she must die
Of sorrow. Yet I saw the idle loom
Still in its place. His sunday garments hung
Upon the self-same nail, his very staff
Stood undisturbed behind the door, and when
I passed this way beaten by Autumn winds
She told me that her little babe was dead
And she was left alone. That very time,
I yet remember, through the miry lane
She walked with me a mile, when the bare trees
Trickled with foggy damps, and in such sort
That any heart had ached to hear her begg'd
That wheresoe'er I went I still would ask
For him whom she had lost. We parted then,
Our final parting, for from that time forth
Did many seasons pass ere I returned
Into this tract again.
                              Five tedious years
She lingered in unquiet widowhood,
A wife and widow. Needs must it have been
A sore heart-wasting. I have heard, my friend,

That in that broken arbour she would sit
The idle length of half a sabbath day—
There, where you see the toadstool's lazy head—
And when a dog passed by she still would quit
The shade and look abroad. On this old Bench
For hours she sate, and evermore her eye
Was busy in the distance, shaping things
Which made her heart beat quick. Seest thou that path?
The green-sward now has broken its grey line;
There to and fro she paced through many a day
Of the warm summer, from a belt of flax
That girt her waist spinning the long-drawn thread
With backward steps.—Yet ever as there passed
A man whose garments shewed the Soldier's red,
Or crippled Mendicant in Sailor's garb,
The little child who sate to turn the wheel
Ceased from his toil, and she with faltering voice,
Expecting still to learn her husband's fate,
Made many a fond inquiry, and when they
Whose presence gave no comfort were gone by,
Her heart was still more sad. And by yon gate
Which bars the traveller's road she often stood
And when a stranger horseman came, the latch
Would lift, and in his face look wistfully,
Most happy if from aught discovered there
Of tender feeling she might dare repeat
The same sad question. Meanwhile her poor hut
Sunk to decay, for he was gone whose hand
At the first nippings of October frost
Closed up each chink and with fresh bands of straw
Chequered the green-grown thatch. And so she lived
Through the long winter, reckless and alone,

Till this reft house by frost, and thaw, and rain
Was sapped, and when she slept the nightly damps
Did chill her breast, and in the stormy day
Her tattered clothes were ruffled by the wind
Even at the side of her own fire. Yet still
She loved this wretched spot, nor would for worlds
Have parted hence, and still that length of road
And this rude bench one torturing hope endeared,
Fast rooted at her heart, and here, my friend,
In sickness she remained, and here she died,
Last human tenant of these ruined walls.'
    The old Man ceased: he saw that I was mov'd;
From that low Bench, rising instinctively,
I turned aside in weakness, nor had power
To thank him for the tale which he had told.
I stood, and leaning o'er the garden-gate
Reviewed that Woman's suff'rings, and it seemed
To comfort me while with a brother's love
I blessed her in the impotence of grief.
At length upon the hut I fix'd my eyes
Fondly, and traced with milder interest
That secret spirit of humanity
Which, 'mid the calm oblivious tendencies
Of nature, 'mid her plants, her weeds, and flowers,
And silent overgrowings, still survived.
The old man, seeing this, resumed and said,
'My Friend, enough to sorrow have you given,
The purposes of wisdom ask no more;
Be wise and chearful, and no longer read
The forms of things with an unworthy eye.
She sleeps in the calm earth, and peace is here.
I well remember that those very plumes,

Those weeds, and the high spear-grass on that wall,
By mist and silent rain-drops silvered o'er,
As once I passed did to my heart convey
So still an image of tranquillity,
So calm and still, and looked so beautiful
Amid the uneasy thoughts which filled my mind,
That what we feel of sorrow and despair
From ruin and from change, and all the grief
The passing shews of being leave behind,
Appeared an idle dream that could not live
Where meditation was. I turned away
And walked along my road in happiness.'
    He ceased. By this the sun declining shot
A slant and mellow radiance which began
To fall upon us where beneath the trees
We sate on that low bench, and now we felt,
Admonished thus, the sweet hour coming on.
A linnet warbled from those lofty elms,
A thrush sang loud, and other melodies,
At distance heard, peopled the milder air.
The old man rose and hoisted up his load.
Together casting then a farewell look
Upon those silent walls, we left the shade
And ere the stars were visible attained
A rustic inn, our evening resting-place.

The End

THE TWO-PART PRELUDE

'Manuscript V' (1798–9)

[heavily revised lines at top, partly illegible]
A Babe — of the beauty of the world ...
though nobly housing at the ...
... & delight ... for ...
... go one use ... what ... for this

That one, the fairest of all rivers, loved
To blend his murmurs with my Nurse's song,
And, from his alder shades, and rocky falls,
And from his fords and shallows, sent a voice
That flowed along my dreams? For this didst thou
O Derwent, travelling over the green plains
Near my "sweet birth-place," didst thou beauteous Stream
Make ceaseless music through the night and day,
Which with its steady cadence, tempering
Our human waywardness, composed my thoughts
To more than infant softness, giving me,
Among the fretful dwellings of mankind,
A knowledge, a dim earnest of the calm,
Which Nature breathes among the fields and groves.
    Beloved Derwent, fairest of all Streams!
Was it for this that I, a four years child,
A naked Boy, among thy silent pools,
Made one long bathing of a summer's day?
Bashed in the sun, or plunged into thy stream,
Alternate, all a summer's day, or coursed
Over the sandy fields, and dashed the flowers
Of yellow grunsel, or when crag and hill,
The woods and distant Skiddaw's lofty height
Were bronzed with a deep radiance, stood alone,
... Savage in the thunder shower?

THE TWO-PART PRELUDE

First Part

Was it for this
That one, the fairest of all rivers, loved
To blend his murmurs with my Nurse's song,
And from his alder shades, and rocky falls,
And from his fords and shallows, sent a voice
That flowed along my dreams? For this didst thou
O Derwent, travelling over the green plains
Near my 'sweet birthplace,' didst thou beauteous Stream,
Make ceaseless music through the night and day,
Which with its steady cadence tempering
Our human waywardness, composed my thoughts
To more than infant softness, giving me,
Among the fretful dwellings of mankind,
A knowledge, a dim earnest of the calm
Which Nature breathes among the fields and groves?
 Beloved Derwent! fairest of all Streams!
Was it for this that I, a four years' child,
A naked Boy, among thy silent pools
Made one long bathing of a summer's day?
Basked in the sun, or plunged into thy streams,
Alternate, all a summer's day, or coursed
Over the sandy fields, and dashed the flowers
Of yellow grunsel, or, when crag and hill,
The woods and distant Skiddaw's lofty height
Were bronzed with a deep radiance, stood alone,
A naked Savage in the thunder shower?
 And afterwards 'twas in a later day
Though early, when upon the mountain-slope

The frost and breath of frosty wind had snapped
The last autumnal crocus, 'twas my joy
To wander half the night among the cliffs
And the smooth hollows, where the woodcocks ran
Along the moonlight turf. In thought and wish,
That time, my shoulder all with springes hung,
I was a fell destroyer. Gentle powers!
Who give us happiness and call it peace!
When scudding on from snare to snare I plied
My anxious visitation, hurrying on,
Still hurrying hurrying onward, how my heart
Panted; among the scattered yew-trees, and the crags
That looked upon me, how my bosom beat
With expectation. Sometimes strong desire
Resistless, overpowered me, and the bird
Which was the captive of another's toils
Became my prey; and when the deed was done
I heard among the solitary hills
Low breathings coming after me, and sounds
Of undistinguishable motion, steps
Almost as silent as the turf they trod.
    Nor less, in spring-time, when on southern banks
The shining sun had from his knot of leaves
Decoyed the primrose-flower, and when the vales
And woods were warm, was I a rover then
In the high places, on the lonesome peaks,
Among the mountains and the winds. Though mean
And though inglorious were my views, the end
Was not ignoble. Oh, when I have hung
Above the raven's nest, by knots of grass,
Or half-inch fissures in the slipp'ry rock,
But ill sustained, and almost, as it seemed,

Suspended by the blast which blew amain
Shouldering the naked crag, Oh, at that time,
While on the perilous ridge I hung alone,
With what strange utterance did the loud dry wind
Blow through my ears, the sky seemed not a sky
Of earth, and with what motion moved the clouds!
    The mind of man is fashioned and built up
Even as a strain of music: I believe
That there are spirits which, when they would form
A favored being, from his very dawn
Of infancy do open out the clouds
As at the touch of lightning, seeking him
With gentle visitation; quiet powers!
Retired and seldom recognized, yet kind,
And to the very meanest not unknown;
With me, though rarely,
They communed: others too there are, who use,
Yet haply aiming at the self-same end,
Severer interventions, ministry
More palpable, and of their school was I.
They guided me: one evening, led by them,
I went alone into a Shepherd's boat,
A skiff that to a willow-tree was tied
Within a rocky cave, its usual home;
The moon was up, the lake was shining clear
Among the hoary mountains: from the shore
I pushed, and struck the oars and struck again
In cadence, and my little Boat moved on
Just like a man who walks with stately step
Though bent on speed. It was an act of stealth
And troubled pleasure; not without the voice
Of mountain echoes did my boat move on,

Leaving behind her still on either side
Small circles glittering idly in the moon
Until they melted all into one track
Of sparkling light. A rocky steep uprose
Above the cavern of the willow tree,
And now, as suited one who proudly rowed
With his best skill, I fixed a steady view
Upon the top of that same craggy ridge,
The bound of the horizon, for behind
Was nothing but the stars and the grey sky.
—She was an elfin pinnace; twenty times
I dipped my oars into the silent lake,
And, as I rose upon the stroke, my Boat
Went heaving through the water, like a swan.
When from behind that rocky steep, till then
The bound of the horizon, a huge Cliff,
As if with voluntary power instinct,
Upreared its head: I struck, and struck again,
And, growing still in stature, the huge cliff
Rose up between me and the stars, and still
With measured motion, like a living thing,
Strode after me. With trembling hands I turned,
And through the silent water stole my way
Back to the cavern of the willow-tree.
There, in her mooring-place I left my bark,
And through the meadows homeward went with grave
And serious thoughts: and after I had seen
That spectacle, for many days my brain
Worked with a dim and undetermined sense
Of unknown modes of being: in my thoughts
There was a darkness, call it solitude
Or blank desertion, no familiar shapes

Of hourly objects, images of trees,
Of sea or sky, no colours of green fields:
But huge and mighty forms, that do not live
Like living men, moved slowly through my mind
By day, and were the trouble of my dreams.

    Ah! not in vain ye Beings of the hills,
And ye that walk the woods and open heaths
By moon or starlight, thus from my first dawn
Of childhood did ye love to intertwine
The passions that build up our human soul
Not with the mean and vulgar works of man
But with high objects, with eternal things,
With life and Nature purifying thus
The elements of feeling and of thought,
And sanctifying by such discipline
Both pain and fear until we recognise
A grandeur in the beatings of the heart.

    Nor was this fellowship vouchsafed to me
With stinted kindness. In November days,
When vapours, rolling down the valleys, made
A lonely scene more lonesome; among woods
At noon, and 'mid the calm of summer nights
When by the margin of the trembling lake
Beneath the gloomy hills I homeward went
In solitude, such intercourse was mine.

    And in the frosty season when the sun
Was set, and, visible for many a mile,
The cottage windows through the twilight blazed,
I heeded not the summons: clear and loud
The village clock tolled six; I wheeled about
Proud and exulting like an untired horse
That cares not for its home—All shod with steel

We hissed along the polished ice, in games
Confederate, imitative of the chace
And woodland pleasures, the resounding horn,
The pack loud bellowing, and the hunted hare.
So through the darkness and the cold we flew,
And not a voice was idle: with the din,
Meanwhile, the precipices rang aloud,
The leafless trees and every icy crag
Tinkled like iron; while the distant hills
Into the tumult sent an alien sound
Of melancholy not unnoticed, while the stars,
Eastward, were sparkling clear, and in the west
The orange sky of evening died away.

   Not seldom from the uproar I retired
Into a silent bay, or sportively
Glanced side-way, leaving the tumultuous throng
To cut across the shadow of a star
That gleamed upon the ice: and oftentimes
When we had given our bodies to the wind,
And all the shadowy banks on either side
Came sweeping through the darkness, spinning still
The rapid line of motion, then at once
Have I, reclining back upon my heels,
Stopped short, yet still the solitary cliffs
Wheeled by me, even as if the earth had rolled
With visible motion her diurnal round.
Behind me did they stretch in solemn train
Feebler and feebler, and I stood and watched
Till all was tranquil as a summer sea.

   Ye Powers of earth! ye Genii of the springs!
And ye that have your voices in the clouds
And ye that are familiars of the lakes

And of the standing pools, I may not think
A vulgar hope was yours when ye employed
Such ministry, when ye through many a year
Thus by the agency of boyish sports
On caves and trees, upon the woods and hills,
Impressed upon all forms the characters
Of danger or desire, and thus did make
The surface of the universal earth
With meanings of delight, of hope and fear,
Work like a sea.
                    Not uselessly employed
I might pursue this theme through every change
Of exercise and sport to which the year
Did summon us in its delightful round.
We were a noisy crew; the sun in heaven
Beheld not vales more beautiful than ours
Nor saw a race in happiness and joy
More worthy of the fields where they were sown.
I would record with no reluctant voice
Our home amusements by the warm peat fire
At evening, when with pencil, and with slate
In square divisions parcelled out, and all
With crosses and with cyphers scribbled o'er
We schemed and puzzled, head opposed to head
In strife too humble to be named in verse;
Or round the naked table, snow-white deal,
Cherry, or maple, sate in close array,
And to the combat—Lu or Whist—led on
A thick-ribbed army, not as in the world
Discarded and ungratefully thrown by
Even for the very service they had wrought,
But husbanded through many a long campaign.

Oh, with what echoes on the board they fell—
Ironic diamonds, hearts of sable hue
Queens gleaming through their splendour's last decay,
Knaves wrapt in one assimilating gloom
And kings indignant at the shame incurred
By royal visages. Meanwhile abroad
The heavy rain was falling, or the frost
Raged bitterly with keen and silent tooth,
And, interrupting the impassioned game,
Oft from the neighbouring lake the splitting ice,
While it sank down towards the water, sent
Among the meadows and the hills its long
And frequent yellings, imitative some
Of wolves that howl along the Bothnic main.
  Nor with less willing heart would I rehearse
The woods of autumn and their hidden bowers
With milk-white clusters hung; the rod and line,
True symbol of the foolishness of hope,
Which with its strong enchantment led me on
By rocks, and pools where never summer star
Impressed its shadow, to forlorn cascades
Among the windings of the mountain-brooks;
The kite in sultry calms from some high hill
Sent up, ascending thence till it was lost
Among the fleecy clouds; in gusty days
Launched from the lower grounds, and suddenly
Dashed headlong—and rejected by the storm.
All these and more with rival claims demand
Grateful acknowledgement. It were a song
Venial, and such as if I rightly judge
I might protract unblamed, but I perceive
That much is overlooked, and we should ill

Attain our object if from delicate fears
Of breaking in upon the unity
Of this my argument I should omit
To speak of such effects as cannot here
Be regularly classed, yet tend no less
To the same point, the growth of mental power
And love of Nature's works.
                                    Ere I had seen
Eight summers (and 'twas in the very week
When I was first transplanted to thy vale,
Beloved Hawkshead! when thy paths, thy shores
And brooks were like a dream of novelty
To my half-infant mind) I chanced to cross
One of those open fields which, shaped like ears,
Make green peninsulas on Esthwaite's lake.
Twilight was coming on, yet through the gloom
I saw distinctly on the opposite shore,
Beneath a tree and close by the lake side,
A heap of garments as if left by one
Who there was bathing: half an hour I watched
And no one owned them: meanwhile the calm lake
Grew dark with all the shadows on its breast,
And now and then a leaping fish disturbed
The breathless stillness. The succeeding day
There came a company, and in their boat
Sounded with iron hooks and with long poles.
At length the dead man, 'mid that beauteous scene
Of trees and hills and water, bolt upright
Rose with his ghastly face. I might advert
To numerous accidents in flood or field,
Quarry or moor, or 'mid the winter snows,
Distresses and disasters, tragic facts

Of rural history, that impressed my mind
With images, to which in following years
Far other feelings were attached; with forms
That yet exist with independent life,
And, like their archetypes, know no decay.
  There are in our existence spots of time
Which with distinct preeminence retain
A fructifying virtue, whence, depressed
By trivial occupations and the round
Of ordinary intercourse, our minds
(Especially the imaginative power)
Are nourished and invisibly repaired.
Such moments chiefly seem to have their date
In our first childhood. I remember well
('Tis of an early season that I speak,
The twilight of rememberable life,)
While I was yet an urchin, one who scarce
Could hold a bridle, with ambitious hopes
I mounted, and we rode towards the hills;
We were a pair of horsemen: honest James
Was with me, my encourager and guide.
We had not travelled long ere some mischance
Disjoined me from my comrade, and through fear
Dismounting, down the rough and stony moor
I led my horse and, stumbling on, at length
Came to a bottom where in former times
A man, the murderer of his wife, was hung
In irons; mouldered was the gibbet-mast;
The bones were gone, the iron and the wood;
Only a long green ridge of turf remained
Whose shape was like a grave. I left the spot,
And, reascending the bare slope, I saw

A naked pool that lay beneath the hills,
The beacon on the summit, and more near
A girl who bore a pitcher on her head
And seemed with difficult steps to force her way
Against the blowing wind. It was in truth
An ordinary sight, but I should need
Colours and words that are unknown to man
To paint the visionary dreariness
Which, while I looked all round for my lost guide,
Did, at that time, invest the naked pool,
The beacon on the lonely eminence,
The woman and her garments vexed and tossed
By the strong wind. Nor less I recollect
(Long after, though my childhood had not ceased)
Another scene which left a kindred power
Implanted in my mind.
       One Christmas-time,
The day before the holidays began,
Feverish, and tired and restless, I went forth
Into the fields, impatient for the sight
Of those three horses which should bear us home,
My brothers and myself. There was a crag,
An eminence, which from the meeting-point
Of two highways ascending overlooked
At least a long half-mile of those two roads,
By each of which the expected steeds might come;
The choice uncertain. Thither I repaired
Up to the highest summit; 'twas a day
Stormy, and rough, and wild, and on the grass
I sate, half sheltered by a naked wall.
Upon my right hand was a single sheep,
A whistling hawthorn on my left, and there,

Those two companions at my side, I watched
With eyes intensely straining as the mist
Gave intermitting prospects of the wood
And plain beneath. Ere I to school returned
That dreary time, ere I had been ten days
A dweller in my Father's house, he died,
And I and my two brothers, orphans then,
Followed his body to the grave. The event,
With all the sorrow which it brought, appeared
A chastisement; and when I called to mind
That day so lately passed, when from the crag
I looked in such anxiety of hope,
With trite reflections of morality
Yet with the deepest passion I bowed low
To God, who thus corrected my desires.
And afterwards the wind, and sleety rain,
And all the business of the elements,
The single sheep, and the one blasted tree,
And the bleak music of that old stone wall,
The noise of wood and water, and the mist
Which on the line of each of those two roads
Advanced in such indisputable shapes—
All these were spectacles and sounds to which
I often would repair, and thence would drink
As at a fountain, and I do not doubt
That in this later time, when storm and rain
Beat on my roof at midnight, or by day
When I am in the woods, unknown to me
The workings of my spirit thence are brought.
                Nor sedulous to trace
How Nature by collateral interest
And by extrinsic passion peopled first

My mind with forms or beautiful or grand
And made me love them, may I well forget
How other pleasures have been mine, and joys
Of subtler origin; how I have felt
Not seldom, even in that tempestuous time,
Those hallowed and pure motions of the sense
Which seem in their simplicity to own
An intellectual charm, that calm delight
Which, if I err not, surely must belong
To those first-born affinities that fit
Our new existence to existing things,
And in our dawn of being constitute
The bond of union betwixt life and joy.

 Yes, I remember when the changeful earth
And twice five seasons on my mind had stamped
The faces of the moving year, even then,
A Child, I held unconscious intercourse
With the eternal Beauty, drinking in
A pure organic pleasure from the lines
Of curling mist, or from the level plain
Of waters coloured by the steady clouds.

 The sands of Westmoreland, the creeks and bays
Of Cumbria's rocky limits, they can tell
How when the sea threw off his evening shade
And to the shepherd's hut beneath the crags
Did send sweet notice of the rising moon,
How I have stood to images like these
A stranger, linking with the spectacle
No body of associated forms
And bringing with me no peculiar sense
Of quietness or peace, yet I have stood
Even while my eye has moved o'er three long leagues

Of shining water, gathering, as it seemed,
Through the wide surface of that field of light
New pleasure, like a bee among the flowers.
    Thus often in those fits of vulgar joy
Which through all seasons on a child's pursuits
Are prompt attendants, 'mid that giddy bliss
Which like a tempest works along the blood
And is forgotten, even then I felt
Gleams like the flashing of a shield; the earth
And common face of Nature spake to me
Rememberable things: sometimes 'tis true
By quaint associations, yet not vain
Nor profitless if haply they impressed
Collateral objects and appearances,
Albeit lifeless then, and doomed to sleep
Until maturer seasons called them forth
To impregnate and to elevate the mind.
—And if the vulgar joy by its own weight
Wearied itself out of the memory,
The scenes which were a witness of that joy
Remained, in their substantial lineaments
Depicted on the brain, and to the eye
Were visible, a daily sight: and thus
By the impressive agency of fear,
By pleasure and repeated happiness,
So frequently repeated, and by force
Of obscure feelings representative
Of joys that were forgotten, these same scenes
So beauteous and majestic in themselves,
Though yet the day was distant, did at length
Become habitually dear, and all

Their hues and forms were by invisible links
Allied to the affections.
                              I began
My story early, feeling, as I fear,
The weakness of a human love for days
Disowned by memory, ere the birth of spring
Planting my snowdrops among winter snows.
Nor will it seem to thee, my Friend, so prompt
In sympathy, that I have lengthened out
With fond and feeble tongue a tedious tale.
Meanwhile my hope has been that I might fetch
Reproaches from my former years, whose power
May spur me on, in manhood now mature,
To honourable toil. Yet, should it be
That this is but an impotent desire,
That I by such inquiry am not taught
To understand myself, nor thou to know
With better knowledge how the heart was framed
Of him thou lovest, need I dread from thee
Harsh judgements if I am so loth to quit
Those recollected hours that have the charm
Of visionary things, and lovely forms
And sweet sensations that throw back our life
And make our infancy a visible scene
On which the sun is shining?

Thus far my Friend, have we retraced the way
Through which I travelled when I first began
To love the woods and fields: the passion yet
Was in its birth, sustained as might befal
By nourishment that came unsought, for still
From week to week, from month to month, we lived
A round of tumult: duly were our games
Prolonged in summer till the day-light failed;
No chair remained before the doors, the bench
And threshold steps were empty, fast asleep
The labourer and the old man who had sate
A later lingerer, yet the revelry
Continued and the loud uproar: at last
When all the ground was dark, and the huge clouds
Were edged with twinkling stars, to bed we went
With weary joints and with a beating mind.
Ah! is there one who ever has been young
And needs a monitory voice to tame
The pride of virtue and of intellect?
And is there one, the wisest and the best
Of all mankind, who does not sometimes wish
For things which cannot be, who would not give,
If so he might, to duty and to truth
The eagerness of infantine desire?
A tranquillizing spirit presses now
On my corporeal frame, so wide appears
The vacancy between me and those days,
Which yet have such self-presence in my heart
That sometimes when I think of them I seem
Two consciousnesses, conscious of myself

And of some other being. A grey stone
Of native rock, left midway in the square
Of our small market-village, was the home
And centre of these joys, and when, returned
After long absence, thither I repaired,
I found that it was split and gone to build
A smart assembly-room that perked and flared
With wash and rough-cast, elbowing the ground
Which had been ours. But let the fiddle scream
And be ye happy! yet I know, my Friends,
That more than one of you will think with me
Of those soft starry nights, and that old dame
From whom the stone was named, who there had sate
And watched her table with its huckster's wares,
Assiduous, for the length of sixty years.
—We ran a boisterous race, the year span round
With giddy motion. But the time approached
That brought with it a regular desire
For calmer pleasures, when the beauteous scenes
Of nature were collaterally attached
To every scheme of holiday delight
And every boyish sport, less grateful else
And languidly pursued.
     When summer came
It was the pastime of our afternoons
To beat along the plain of Windermere
With rival oars; and the selected bourn
Was now an island musical with birds
That sang for ever; now a sister isle
Beneath the oak's umbrageous' covert sown
With lilies-of-the-valley like a field,
And now a third small island where remained

An old stone table and one mouldered cave,
A hermit's history. In such a race,
So ended, disappointment could be none,
Uneasiness, or pain, or jealousy;
We rested in the shade, all pleased alike,
Conquered or conqueror. Thus our selfishness
Was mellowed down, and thus the pride of strength
And the vainglory of superior skill
Were interfused with objects which subdued
And tempered them, and gradually produced
A quiet independence of the heart.
And to my Friend who knows me I may add,
Unapprehensive of reproof, that hence
Ensued a diffidence and modesty,
And I was taught to feel, perhaps too much,
The self-sufficing power of solitude.
    No delicate viands sapped our bodily strength;
More than we wished we knew the blessing then
Of vigorous hunger, for our daily meals
Were frugal, Sabine fare! and then exclude
A little weekly stipend, and we lived
Through three divisions of the quartered year
In pennyless poverty. But now to school
Returned from the half-yearly holidays,
We came with purses more profusely filled,
Allowance which abundantly sufficed
To gratify the palate with repasts
More costly than the Dame of whom I spake,
That ancient woman, and her board, supplied.
Hence inroads into distant vales, and long
Excursions far away among the hills,
Hence rustic dinners on the cool green ground,

Or in the woods, or by a river-side
Or fountain, festive banquets that provoked
The languid action of a natural scene
By pleasure of corporeal appetite.
    Nor is my aim neglected if I tell
How twice in the long length of those half years
We from our funds perhaps with bolder hand
Drew largely, anxious for one day at least
To feel the motion of the galloping steed;
And with the good old Innkeeper in truth
I needs must say that sometimes we have used
Sly subterfuge, for the intended bound
Of the day's journey was too distant far
For any cautious man, a structure famed
Beyond its neighbourhood, the antique walls
Of a large Abbey, with its fractured arch,
Belfry, and images, and living trees,
A holy scene! Along the smooth green turf
Our horses grazed: in more than inland peace,
Left by the winds that overpass the vale
In that sequestered ruin trees and towers,
Both silent and both motionless alike,
Hear all day long the murmuring sea that beats
Incessantly upon a craggy shore.
    Our steeds remounted, and the summons given
With whip and spur we by the chantry flew
In uncouth race; and left the cross-legged Knight
And the stone Abbot, and that single wren
Which one day sang so sweetly in the nave
Of the old church that, though from recent showers
The earth was comfortless, and, touched by faint
Internal breezes from the roofless walls

The shuddering ivy dripped large drops, yet still
So sweetly 'mid the gloom the invisible bird
Sang to itself that there I could have made
My dwelling-place, and lived for ever there
To hear such music. Through the walls we flew
And down the valley, and, a circuit made
In wantonness of heart, through rough and smooth
We scampered homeward. O ye rocks and streams,
And that still spirit of the evening air,
Even in this joyous time I sometimes felt
Your presence when with slackened step we breathed
Along the sides of the steep hills, or when,
Lightened by gleams of moonlight from the sea,
We beat with thundering hoofs the level sand.
  There was a row of ancient trees, since fallen,
That on the margin of a jutting land
Stood near the lake of Coniston, and made
With its long boughs above the water stretched
A gloom through which a boat might sail along
As in a cloister. An old Hall was near,
Grotesque and beautiful, its gavel-end
And huge round chimneys to the top o'ergrown
With fields of ivy. Thither we repaired,
'Twas even a custom with us, to the shore
And to that cool piazza. They who dwelt
In the neglected mansion-house supplied
Fresh buttter, tea-kettle and earthen-ware,
And chafing-dish with smoking coals, and so
Beneath the trees we sate in our small boat,
And in the covert eat our delicate meal
Upon the calm smooth lake. It was a joy
Worthy the heart of one who is full grown

To rest beneath those horizontal boughs
And mark the radiance of the setting sun,
Himself unseen, reposing on the top
Of the high eastern hills. And there I said,
That beauteous sight before me, there I said,
(Then first beginning in my thoughts to mark
That sense of dim similitude which links
Our moral feelings with extemal forms)
That in whatever region I should close
My mortal life I would remember you
Fair scenes! that dying I would think on you,
My soul would send a longing look to you:
Even as that setting sun, while all the vale
Could nowhere catch one faint memorial gleam,
Yet with the last remains of his last light
Still lingered, and a farewell lustre threw
On the dear mountain-tops where first he rose.
    'Twas then my fourteenth summer, and these words
Were uttered in a casual access
Of sentiment, a momentary trance
That far outran the habit of my mind.
    Upon the eastern shore of Windermere
Above the crescent of a pleasant Bay,
There was an Inn, no homely-featured shed
Brother of the surrounding cottages,
But 'twas a splendid place, the door beset
With chaises, grooms, and liveries, and within
Decanters, glasses, and the blood-red wine.
In ancient times, or ere the hall was built
On the large island, had the dwelling been
More worthy of a poet's love, a hut
Proud of its one bright fire and sycamore shade;

But though the rhymes were gone which once inscribed
The threshold, and large golden characters
On the blue-frosted signboard had usurped
The place of the old Lion in contempt
And mockery of the rustic painter's hand,
Yet to this hour the spot to me is dear
With all its foolish pomp. The garden lay
Upon a slope surmounted by the plain
Of a small bowling-green; beneath us stood
A grove, with gleams of water through the trees
And over the tree-tops; nor did we want
Refreshment, strawberries and mellow cream,
And there through half an afternoon we played
On the smooth platform, and the shouts we sent
Made all the mountains ring. But ere the fall
Of night, when in our pinnace we returned
Over the dusky lake, and to the beach
Of some small island steered our course with one,
The minstrel of our troop, and left him there,
And rowed off gently, while he blew his flute
Alone upon the rock; oh then the calm
And dead still water lay upon my mind
Even with a weight of pleasure, and the sky,
Never before so beautiful, sank down
Into my heart and held me like a dream.

    Thus day by day my sympathies increased
And thus the common range of visible things
Grew dear to me: already I began
To love the sun, a Boy I loved the sun
Not, as I since have loved him, as a pledge
And surety of my earthly life, a light
Which while I view I feel I am alive,

But for this cause, that I had seen him lay
His beauty on the morning hills, had seen
The western mountain touch his setting orb
In many a thoughtless hour, when from excess
Of happiness my blood appeared to flow
With its own pleasure and I breathed with joy.
And from like feelings, humble though intense,
To patriotic and domestic love
Analogous, the moon to me was dear,
For I would dream away my purposes
Standing to look upon her, while she hung
Midway between the hills as if she knew
No other region but belonged to thee,
Yea, appertained by a peculiar right
To thee and thy grey huts, my native vale.

    Those incidental charms which first attached
My heart to rural objects day by day
Grew weaker, and I hasten on to tell
How Nature, intervenient till this time
And secondary, now at length was sought
For her own sake.—But who shall parcel out
His intellect by geometric rules,
Split like a province into round and square;
Who knows the individual hour in which
His habits were first sown even as a seed;
Who that shall point as with a wand, and say,
This portion of the river of my mind
Came from yon fountain? Thou, my Friend, art one
More deeply read in thy own thoughts, no slave
Of that false secondary power by which
In weakness we create distinctions, then
Believe our puny boundaries are things

Which we perceive, and not which we have made.
To thee, unblinded by these outward shews,
The unity of all has been revealed,
And thou wilt doubt with me, less aptly skilled
Than many are to class the cabinet
Of their sensations, and in voluble phrase
Run through the history and birth of each
As of a single independent thing.
Hard task to analyse a soul in which
Not only general habits and desires,
But each most obvious and particular thought,
Not in a mystical and idle sense,
But in the words of reason deeply weighed,
Hath no beginning.
                        Blessed the infant babe
(For my best conjectures I would trace
The progress of our being) blest the Babe
Nursed in his Mother's arms, the Babe who sleeps
Upon his mother's breast, who when his soul
Claims manifest kindred with an earthly soul
Doth gather passion from his mother's eye.
Such feelings pass into his torpid life
Like an awakening breeze, and hence his mind
Even in the first trial of its powers
Is prompt and watchful, eager to combine
In one appearance all the elements
And parts of the same object, else detached
And loth to coalesce. Thus day by day
Subjected to the discipline of love
His organs and recipient faculties
Are quickened, are more vigorous; his mind spreads,
Tenacious of the forms which it receives.

In one beloved presence, nay and more,
In that most apprehensive habitude
And those sensations which have been derived
From this beloved presence, there exists
A virtue which irradiates and exalts
All objects through all intercourse of sense.
No outcast he, bewildered and depressed;
Along his infant veins are interfused
The gravitation and the filial bond
Of Nature that connect him with the world.
Emphatically such a being lives
An inmate of this *active* universe.
From Nature largely he receives, nor so
Is satisfied, but largely gives again;
For feeling has to him imparted strength,
And powerful in all sentiments of grief,
Of exultation, fear and joy, his mind,
Even as an agent of the one great mind,
Creates, creator and receiver both,
Working but in alliance with the works
Which it beholds.—Such verily is the first
Poetic spirit of our human life,
By uniform control of after years
In most abated and suppressed, in some
Through every change of growth or of decay
Preeminent till death.
                 From early days,
Beginning not long after that first time
In which, a Babe, by intercourse of touch
I held mute dialogues with my mother's heart,
I have endeavoured to display the means
Whereby this infant sensibility,

Great birth-right of our being, was in me
Augmented and sustained. Yet is a path
More difficult before me, and I fear
That in its broken windings we shall need
The Chamois' sinews and the eagle's wing,
For now a trouble came into my mind
From   causes. I was left alone
Seeking this visible world, nor knowing why.
The props of my affections were removed,
And yet the building stood as if sustained
By its own spirit. All that I beheld
Was dear to me, and from this cause it came
That now to Nature's finer influxes
My mind lay open to that more exact
And intimate communion which our hearts
Maintain with the minuter properties
Of objects which already are beloved,
And of those only. Many are the joys
Of youth but oh! what happiness to live
When every hour brings palpable access
Of knowledge, when all knowledge is delight
And sorrow is not there. The seasons came,
And every season brought a countless store
Of modes and temporary qualities
Which, but for this most watchful power of love,
Had been neglected, left a register
Of permanent relations else unknown.
Hence life, and change, and beauty, solitude
More active even than 'best society',
Society made sweet as solitude
By silent inobtrusive sympathies,
And gentle agitations of the mind

From manifold distinctions, difference
Perceived in things where to the common eye
No difference is: and hence from the same source
Sublimer joy; for I would walk alone
In storm and tempest or in starlight nights
Beneath the quiet heavens, and at that time
Would feel whate'er there is of power in sound
To breathe an elevated mood by form
Or image unprofaned: and I would stand
Beneath some rock listening to sounds that are
The ghostly language of the ancient earth,
Or make their dim abode in distant winds.
Thence did I drink the visionary power.
I deem not profitless these fleeting moods
Of shadowy exaltation, not for this
That they are kindred to our purer mind
And intellectual life, but that the soul
Remembering how she felt, but what she felt
Remembering not, retains an obscure sense
Of possible sublimity, to which
With growing faculties she doth aspire,
With faculties still growing, feeling still
That whatsoever point they gain they still
Have something to pursue.
                              And not alone
In grandeur and in tumult, but no less
In tranquil scenes, that universal power
And fitness in the latent qualities
And essences of things by which the mind
Is moved with feelings of delight, to me
Came strengthened with a superadded soul,
A virtue not its own. My morning walks

Were early; oft before the hours of school
I travelled round our little lake, five miles
Of pleasant wandering, happy time, more dear
For this, that one was by my side, a Friend
Then passionately loved; with heart how full
Will he peruse these lines, this page, perhaps
A blank to other men, for many years
Have since flowed in between us, and, our minds
Both silent to each other, at this time
We live as if those hours had never been.
Nor seldom did I lift our cottage latch
Far earlier, and before the vernal thrush
Was audible, among the hills I sate
Alone upon some jutting eminence
At the first hour of morning, when the vale
Lay quiet in an utter solitude.
How shall I trace the history, where seek
The origin of what I then have felt?
Oft in those moments such a holy calm
Did overspread my soul that I forgot
The agency of sight, and what I saw
Appeared like something in myself—a dream,
A prospect in my mind. 'Twere long to tell
What spring and autumn, what the winter snows,
And what the summer-shade, what day and night,
The evening and the morning, what my dreams
And what my waking thoughts, supplied to nurse
That spirit of religious love in which
I walked with nature. But let this at least
Be not forgotten, that I still retained
My first creative sensibility
That by the regular action of the world

My soul was unsubdued. A plastic power
Abode with me, a forming hand, at times
Rebellious, acting in a devious mood,
A local spirit of its own, at war
With general tendency, but for the most
Subservient strictly to the external things
With which it communed. An auxiliar light
Came from my mind which on the setting sun
Bestowed new splendour; the melodious birds
The gentle breezes, fountains that ran on
Murmuring so sweetly in themselves, obeyed
A like dominion, and the midnight storm
Grew darker in the presence of my eye.
Hence my obeisance, my devotion hence,
And *hence* my transport.
                              Nor should this perchance
Pass unrecorded, that I still had loved
The exercise and produce of a toil
Than analytic industry to me
More pleasing, and whose character I deem
Is more poetic, as resembling more
Creative agency—I mean to speak
Of that interminable building reared
By observation of affinities
In objects where no brotherhood exists
To common minds. My seventeenth year was come,
And whether from this habit rooted now
So deeply in my mind, or from excess
Of the great social principle of life
Coercing all things into sympathy,
To unorganic natures I transferred
My own enjoyments, or, the power of truth

Coming in revelation, I conversed
With things that really are, [I at this time]
Saw blessings spread around me like a sea.
Thus did my days pass on, and now at length
From Nature and her overflowing soul
I had received so much that all my thoughts
Were steeped in feeling; I was only then
Contented when with bliss ineffable
I felt the sentiment of being spread
O'er all that moves, and all that seemeth still,
O'er all that, lost beyond the reach of thought
And human knowledge, to the human eye
Invisible, yet liveth to the heart,
O'er all that leaps, and runs, and shouts and sings,
Or beats the gladsome air, o'er all that glides
Beneath the wave, yea, in the wave itself
And mighty depth of waters: wonder not
If such my transports were, for in all things
I saw one life and felt that it was joy.
One song they sang, and it was audible,
Most audible then when the fleshly ear,
O'ercome by grosser prelude of that strain,
Forgot its functions, and slept undisturbed.
    If this be error, and another faith
Find easier access to the pious mind,
Yet were I grossly destitute of all
Those human sentiments which make this earth
[So dear] if I should fail with grateful voice
[To speak of] you, ye mountains! and ye lakes
And sounding cataracts! ye mists and winds
That dwell among the hills where I was born.
If, in my youth, I have been pure in heart,

[148]

If, mingling with the world, I am content
With my own modest pleasures, and have lived
With God and Nature communing, removed
From little enmities and low desires
The gift is yours: if in these times of fear,
This melancholy waste of hopes o'erthrown,
If, 'mid indifference and apathy
And wicked exultation, when good men
On every side fall off we know not how
To selfishness disguised in gentle names
Of peace and quiet and domestic love,
Yet mingled, not unwillingly, with sneers
On visionary minds; if, in this time
Of dereliction and dismay, I yet
Despair not of our nature, but retain
A more than Roman confidence, a faith
That fails not, in all sorrow my support,
The blessing of my life, the gift is yours
Ye mountains! thine O Nature! Thou hast fed
My lofty speculations, and in thee
For this uneasy heart of ours I find
A never-failing principle of joy
And purest passion.
            Thou, my Friend, wast reared
In the great city, 'mid far other scenes,
But we, by different roads, at length have gained
The self-same bourne. And from this cause to thee
I speak unapprehensive of contempt,
The insinuated scoff of coward tongues
And all that silent language which so oft
In conversation betwixt man and man
Blots from the human countenance all trace

Of beauty and of love. For thou hast sought
The truth in solitude, and thou art one
The most intense of Nature's worshippers,
In many things my brother, chiefly here
In this my deep devotion.
                              Fare thee well!
Health and the quiet of a healthful mind
Attend thee! seeking oft the haunts of men
But yet more often living with thyself,
And for thyself, so haply shall thy days
Be many and a blessing to mankind.

End of the second Part.

FROM

LYRICAL BALLADS

(1800)

LYRICAL BALLADS,

OTHER POEMS.

IN TWO VOLUMES.

By W. WORDSWORTH.

———————

Quam nihil ad genium, Papiniane, tuum!

VOL. II.

PRINTED FOR T. N. LONGMAN AND O. REES, PATERNOSTER-ROW,
BY BIGGS AND CO. BRISTOL.

1800.

There was a Boy, ye knew him well, ye Cliffs
And Islands of Winander! many a time,
At evening, when the stars had just begun
To move along the edges of the hills,
Rising or setting, would he stand alone,
Beneath the trees, or by the glimmering lake,
And there, with fingers interwoven, both hands
Pressed closely palm to palm and to his mouth
Uplifted, he, as through an instrument,
Blew mimic hootings to the silent owls
That they might answer him. And they would shout
Across the wat'ry vale and shout again
Responsive to his call, with quivering peals,
And long halloos, and screams, and echoes loud
Redoubled and redoubled, a wild scene
Of mirth and jocund din. And, when it chanced
That pauses of deep silence mocked his skill,
Then, sometimes, in that silence, while he hung
Listening, a gentle shock of mild surprize
Has carried far into his heart the voice
Of mountain torrents, or the visible scene
Would enter unawares into his mind
With all its solemn imagery, its rocks,
Its woods, and that uncertain heaven, received
Into the bosom of the steady lake.

Fair are the woods, and beauteous is the spot,
The vale where he was born: the Church-yard hangs
Upon a slope above the village school,

And there along that bank when I have passed
At evening, I believe, that near his grave
A full half-hour together I have stood,
Mute—for he died when he was ten years old.

THE BROTHERS,*

a Pastoral Poem.

These Tourists, Heaven preserve us! needs must live
A profitable life: some glance along,
Rapid and gay, as if the earth were air.
And they were butterflies to wheel about
Long as their summer lasted; some, as wise,
Upon the forehead of a jutting crag
Sit perched with book and pencil on their knee,
And look and scribble, scribble on and look,
Until a man might travel twelve stout miles,
Or reap an acre of his neighbour's corn.
But, for that moping son of Idleness
Why can he tarry *yonder*?—In our church-yard
Is neither epitaph nor monument,
Tomb-stone nor name, only the turf we tread,
And a few natural graves. To Jane, his Wife,
Thus spake the homely Priest of Ennerdale.
It was a July evening, and he sate
Upon the long stone seat beneath the eaves
Of his old cottage, as it chanced that day,
Employed in winter's work. Upon the stone
His Wife sate near him, teasing matted wool,
While, from the twin cards toothed with glittering wire,
He fed the spindle of his youngest child,
Who turned her large round wheel in the open air
With back and forward steps. Towards the field

* This Poem was intended to be the concluding poem of a series
of pastorals, the scene of which was laid among the mountains of
Cumberland and Westmoreland. I mention this to apologise for the
abruptness with which the poem begins.

In which the parish chapel stood alone,
Girt round with a bare ring of mossy wall,
While half an hour went by, the Priest had sent
Many a long look of wonder, and at last,
Risen from his seat, beside the snow-white ridge
Of carded wool which the old Man had piled
He laid his implements with gentle care,
Each in the other locked; and, down the path
Which from his cottage to the church-yard led,
He took his way, impatient to accost
The Stranger, whom he saw still lingering there.

    'Twas one well known to him in former days,
A Shepherd-lad: who ere his thirteenth year
Had changed his calling, with the mariners
A fellow-mariner, and so had fared
Through twenty seasons; but he had been reared
Among the mountains, and he in his heart
Was half a Shepherd on the stormy seas.
Oft in the piping shrouds had Leonard heard
The tones of waterfalls, and inland sounds
Of caves and trees; and when the regular wind
Between the tropics filled the steady sail
And blew with the same breath through days and weeks,
Lengthening invisibly its weary line
Along the cloudless main, he, in those hours
Of tiresome indolence would often hang
Over the vessel's side, and gaze and gaze,
And, while the broad green wave and sparkling foam
Flashed round him images and hues, that wrought
In union with the employment of his heart,
He, thus by feverish passion overcome,

Even with the organs of his bodily eye,
Below him, in the bosom of the deep
Saw mountains, saw the forms of sheep that grazed
On verdant hills, with dwellings among trees,
And Shepherds clad in the same country grey
Which he himself had worn.*
                                    And now at length,
From perils manifold, with some small wealth
Acquired by traffic in the Indian Isles,
To his paternal home he is returned,
With a determined purpose to resume
The life which he lived there, both for the sake
Of many darling pleasures, and the love
Which to an only brother he has borne
In all his hardships, since that happy time
When, whether it blew foul or fair, they two
Were brother Shepherds on their native hills.
—They were the last of all their race; and now,
When Leonard had approached his home, his heart
Failed in him, and, not venturing to inquire
Tidings of one whom he so dearly loved,
Towards the church-yard he had turned aside,
That, as he knew in what particular spot
His family were laid, he thence might learn
If still his Brother lived, or to the file
Another grave was added.—He had found
Another grave, near which a full half hour
He had remained, but, as he gazed, there grew
Such a confusion in his memory,

* This description of the Calenture is sketched from an imperfect
recollection of an admirable one in prose, by Mr. Gilbert, Author of
the Hurricane.

[157]

That he began to doubt, and he had hopes
That he had seen this heap of turf before,
That it was not another grave, but one,
He had forgotten. He had lost his path,
As up the vale he came that afternoon,
Through fields which once had been well known to him.
And Oh! what joy the recollection now
Sent to his heart! he lifted up his eyes,
And looking round he thought that he perceived
Strange alteration wrought on every side
Among the woods and fields, and that the rocks,
And the eternal hills, themselves were changed.

    By this the Priest who down the field had come
Unseen by Leonard, at the church-yard gate
Stopped short, and thence, at leisure, limb by limb
He scanned him with a gay complacency.
Aye, thought the Vicar, smiling to himself,
'Tis one of those who needs must leave the path
Of the world's business, to go wild alone:
His arms have a perpetual holiday,
The happy man will creep about the fields
Following his fancies by the hour, to bring
Tears down his cheek, or solitary smiles
Into his face, until the setting sun
Write Fool upon his forehead. Planted thus
Beneath a shed that overarched the gate
Of this rude church-yard, till the stars appeared
The good man might have communed with himself
But that the Stranger, who had left the grave,
Approached; he recognized the Priest at once,

And after greetings interchanged, and given
By Leonard to the Vicar as to one
Unknown to him, this dialogue ensued.

LEONARD.

You live, Sir, in these dales, a quiet life:
Your years make up one peaceful family;
And who would grieve and fret, if, welcome come
And welcome gone, they are so like each other,
They cannot be remembered. Scarce a funeral
Comes to this church-yard once in eighteen months;
And yet, some changes must take place among you.
And you, who dwell here, even among these rocks
Can trace the finger of mortality,
And see, that with our threescore years and ten
We are not all that perish.—I remember,
For many years ago I passed this road,
There was a foot-way all along the fields
By the brook-side—'tis gone—and that dark cleft!
To me it does not seem to wear the face
Which then it had.

PRIEST.

Why, Sir, for aught I know,
That chasm is much the same—

LEONARD.

But, surely, yonder—

PRIEST.

Aye, there indeed, your memory is a friend
That does not play you false.—On that tall pike,
(It is the loneliest place of all these hills)
There were two Springs which bubbled side by side,
As if they had been made that they might be

Companions for each other: ten years back,
Close to those brother fountains, the huge crag
Was rent with lightning—one is dead and gone,
The other, left behind, is flowing still.—
For accidents and changes such as these,
Why we have store of them! a water-spout
Will bring down half a mountain; what a feast
For folks that wander up and down like you,
To see an acre's breadth of that wide cliff
One roaring cataract—a sharp May storm
Will come with loads of January snow,
And in one night send twenty score of sheep
To feed the ravens, or a Shepherd dies
By some untoward death among the rocks:
The ice breaks up and sweeps away a bridge—
A wood is felled:—and then for our own homes!
A child is born or christened, a field ploughed,
A daughter sent to service, a web spun,
The old house-clock is decked with a new face;
And hence, so far from wanting facts or dates
To chronicle the time, we all have here
A pair of diaries, one serving, Sir,
For the whole dale, and one for each fire-side,
Yours was a stranger's judgment: for historians
Commend me to these vallies.
                    LEONARD.
                              Yet your church-yard
Seems, if such freedom may be used with you,
To say that you are heedless of the past.
Here's neither head nor foot-stone, plate of brass,
An orphan could nt find his mother's grave:
Cross-bones or skull, type of our earthly state

Or emblem of our hopes: the dead man's home
Is but a fellow to that pasture field.
                    PRIEST.
Why there, Sir, is a thought that's new to me.
The Stone-cutters, 'tis true, might beg their bread
If every English church-yard were like ours:
Yet your conclusion wanders from the truth.
We have no need of names and epitaphs,
We talk about the dead by our fire-sides.
And then for our immortal part, *we* want
No symbols, Sir, to tell us that plain tale:
The thought of death sits easy on the man
Who has been born and dies among the mountains:
                    LEONARD.
Your dalesmen, then, do in each other's thoughts
Possess a kind of second life: no doubt
You, Sir, could help me to the history
Of half these Graves?
                    PRIEST.
                          For eight-score winters past
With what I've witnessed; and with what I've heard,
Perhaps I might, and, on a winter's evening,
If you were seated at my chimney's nook
By turning o'er these hillocks one by one,
We two could travel, Sir, through a strange round,
Yet all in the broad high-way of the world.
Now there's a grave—your foot is half upon it,
It looks just like the rest, and yet that man
Died broken-hearted.
                    LEONARD.
                          'Tis a common case,
We'll take another: who is he that lies

Beneath yon ridge, the last of those three graves;—
It touches on that piece of native rock
Left in the church-yard wall.
                    PRIEST.
                That's Walter Ewbank.
He had as white a head and fresh a cheek
As ever were produced by youth and age
Engendering in the blood of hale fourscore.
For five long generations had the heart
Of Walter's forefathers o'erflowed the bounds
Of their inheritance, that single cottage,
You see it yonder, and those few green fields.
They toiled and wrought, and still, from sire to son,
Each struggled, and each yielded as before
A little—yet a little—and old Walter,
They left to him the family heart, and land
With other burthens than the crop it bore.
Year after year the old man still preserved
A chearful mind, and buffeted with bond,
Interest and mortgages; at last he sank,
And went into his grave before his time.
Poor Walter! whether it was care that spurred him
God only knows, but to the very last
He had the lightest foot in Ennerdale:
His pace was never that of an old man:
I almost see him tripping down the path
With his two Grandsons after him—but you,
Unless our Landlord be your host to-night,
Have far to travel, and in these rough paths
Even in the longest day of midsummer—
                    LEONARD.
But these two Orphans!

PRIEST.
                    Orphans! such they were—
Yet not while Walter lived—for, though their Parents
Lay buried side by side as now they lie,
The old Man was a father to the boys,
Two fathers in one father: and if tears
Shed, when he talked of them where they were not,
And hauntings from the infirmity of love,
Are aught of what makes up a mother's heart,
This old Man in the day of his old age
Was half a mother to them.—If you weep, Sir,
To hear a stranger talking about strangers,
Heaven bless you when you are among your kindred!
Aye. You may turn that way—it is a grave
Which will bear looking at.
                    LEONARD.
                                These Boys I hope
They loved this good old Man—
                    PRIEST.
                                They did—and truly,
But that was what we almost overlooked,
They were such darlings of each other. For
Though from their cradles they had lived with Walter,
The only kinsman near them in the house,
Yet he being old, they had much love to spare,
And it all went into each other's hearts.
Leonard, the elder by just eighteen months,
Was two years taller: 'twas a joy to see,
To hear, to meet them! from their house the School
Was distant three short miles, and in the time
Of storm and thaw, when every water-course
And unbridged stream, such as you may have noticed

Crossing our roads at every hundred steps,
Was swoln into a noisy rivulet,
Would Leonard then, when elder boys perhaps
Remained at home, go staggering through the fords
Bearing his Brother on his back.—I've seen him,
On windy days, in one of those stray brooks,
Aye, more than once I've seen him mid-leg deep,
Their two books lying both on a dry stone
Upon the hither side:—and once I said,
As I remember, looking round these rocks
And hills on which we all of us were born,
That God who made the great book of the world
Would bless such piety—
                    LEONARD.
                              It may be then—
                    PRIEST.
Never did worthier lads break English bread:
The finest Sunday that the Autumn saw,
With all its mealy clusters of ripe nuts,
Could never keep these boys away from church,
Or tempt them to an hour of sabbath breach.
Leonard and James! I warrant, every corner
Among these rocks and every hollow place
Where foot could come, to one or both of them
Was known as well as to the flowers that grow there.
Like roe-bucks they went bounding o'er the hills:
They played like two young ravens on the crags:
Then they could write, aye and speak too, as well
As many of their betters—and for Leonard!
The very night before he went away,
In my own house I put into his hand

A Bible, and I'd wager twenty pounds,
That, if he is alive, he has it yet.

                    LEONARD.

It seems, these Brothers have not lived to be
A comfort to each other.—

                    PRIEST.

                            That they might
Live to that end, is what both old and young
In this our valley all of us have wished,
And what, for my part, I have often prayed:
But Leonard—

                    LEONARD.

                Then James still is left among you—

                    PRIEST.

'Tis of the elder Brother I am speaking:
They had an Uncle, he was at that time
A thriving man, and trafficked on the seas:
And, but for this same Uncle, to this hour
Leonard had never handled rope or shroud.
For the Boy loved the life which we lead here;
And, though a very Stripling, twelve years old;
His soul was knit to this his native soil.
But, as I said, old Walter was too weak
To strive with such a torrent; when he died,
The estate and house were sold, and all their sheep,
A pretty flock, and which, for aught I know,
Had clothed the Ewbanks for a thousand years.
Well—all was gone, and they were destitute.
And Leonard, chiefly for his brother's sake,
Resolved to try his fortune on the seas.
'Tis now twelve years since we had tidings from him.

If there was one among us who had heard
That Leonard Ewbank was come home again,
From the great Gavel,* down by Leeza's Banks,
And down the Enna, far as Egremont,
The day would be a very festival,
And those two bells of ours, which there you see
Hanging in the open air—but, O good Sir!
This is sad talk—they'll never sound for him
Living or dead—When last we heard of him
He was in slavery among the Moors
Upon the Barbary Coast—'Twas not a little
That would bring down his spirit, and, no doubt,
Before it ended in his death, the Lad
Was sadly crossed—Poor Leonard! when we parted,
He took me by the hand and said to me,
If ever the day came when he was rich,
He would return, and on his Father's Land
He would grow old among us.
                    LEONARD.
                              If that day
Should come, 'twould needs be a glad day for him;
He would himself, no doubt, be happy then
As any that should meet him—
                    PRIEST.
                              Happy, Sir—

* The great Gavel, so called I imagine, from its resemblance to
the Gable end of a house, is one of the highest of the Cumberland
mountains. It stands at the head of the several vales of Ennerdale,
Wastdale, and Borrowdale.
    The Leeza is a River which follows into the Lake of Ennerdale:
on issuing from the Lake, it changes its name, and is called the
End, Eyne, or Enna. It falls into the sea a little below Egremont.

LEONARD.

You said his kindred all were in their graves,
And that he had one Brother—

PRIEST.

That is but
A fellow tale of sorrow. From his youth
James, though not sickly, yet was delicate,
And Leonard being always by his side
Had done so many offices about him,
That, though he was not of a timid nature,
Yet still the spirit of a mountain boy
In him was somewhat checked, and when his Brother
Was gone to sea and he was left alone
The little colour that he had was soon
Stolen from his cheek, he drooped, and pined and pined:

LEONARD.

But these are all the graves of full grown men!

PRIEST.

Aye, Sir, that passed away: we took him to us.
He was the child of all the dale—he lived
Three months with one, and six months with another:
And wanted neither food, nor clothes, nor love,
And many, many happy days were his.
But, whether blithe or sad, 'tis my belief
His absent Brother still was at his heart.
And, when he lived beneath our roof, we found
(A practice till this time unknown to him)
That often, rising from his bed at night,
He in his sleep would walk about, and sleeping
He sought his Brother Leonard—You are moved!
Forgive me, Sir: before I spoke to you,
I judged you most unkindly.

LEONARD.

But this youth,
How did he die at last?

PRIEST.

One sweet May morning,
It will be twelve years since, when Spring returns,
He had gone forth among the new-dropped lambs,
With two or three companions whom it chanced
Some further business summoned to a house
Which stands at the Dale-head. James, tired perhaps,
Or from some other cause remained behind.
You see yon precipice—it almost looks
Like some vast building made of many crags,
And in the midst is one particular rock
That rises like a column from the vale,
Whence by our Shepherds it is called, the Pillar.
James pointed to its summit, over which
They all had purposed to return together,
And told them that he there would wait for them:
They parted, and his comrades passed that way
Some two hours after, but they did not find him
At the appointed place, a circumstance
Of which they took no heed: but one of them,
Going by chance, at night, into the house
Which at this time was James's home, there learned
That nobody had seen him all that day:
The morning came, and still, he was unheard of:
The neighbours were alarmed, and to the Brook
Some went, and some towards the Lake; ere noon
They found him at the foot of that same Rock
Dead, and with mangled limbs. The third day after
I buried him, poor Lad, and there he lies.

LEONARD.

And that then *is* his grave!—Before his death
You said that he saw many happy years?

PRIEST.

Aye, that he did—

LEONARD.

And all went well with him—

PRIEST.

If he had one, the Lad had twenty homes.

LEONARD.

And you believe then, that his mind was easy—

PRIEST.

Yes, long before he died, he found that time
Is a true friend to sorrow, and unless
His thoughts were turned on Leonard's luckless fortune,
He talked about him with a chearful love.

LEONARD.

He could not come to an unhallowed end!

PRIEST.

Nay, God forbid! You recollect I mentioned
A habit which disquietude and grief
Had brought upon him, and we all conjectured
That, as the day was warm, he had lain down
Upon the grass, and, waiting for his comrades
He there had fallen asleep, that in his sleep
He to the margin of the precipice
Had walked, and from the summit had fallen head-long,
And so no doubt he perished: at the time,
We guess, that in his hands he must have had
His Shepherd's staff; for midway in the cliff
It had been caught, and there for many years
It hung—and mouldered there.

The Priest here ended—
The Stranger would have thanked him, but he felt
Tears rushing in; both left the spot in silence,
And Leonard, when they reached the church-yard gate,
As the Priest lifted up the latch, turned round,
And, looking at the grave, he said, 'My Brother.'
The Vicar did not hear the words: and now,
Pointing towards the Cottage, he entreated
That Leonard would partake his homely fare:
The other thanked him with a fervent voice,
But added, that, the evening being calm,
He would pursue his journey. So they parted.

It was not long ere Leonard reached a grove
That overhung the road: he there stopped short,
And, sitting down beneath the trees, reviewed
All that the Priest had said: his early years
Were with him in his heart: his cherished hopes,
And thoughts which had been his an hour before,
All pressed on him with such a weight, that now,
This vale, where he had been so happy, seemed
A place in which he could not bear to live:
So he relinquished all his purposes.
He travelled on to Egremont; and thence,
That night, addressed a letter to the Priest
Reminding him of what had passed between them.
And adding, with a hope to be forgiven,
That it was from the weakness of his heart,
He had not dared to tell him, who he was.

This done, he went on shipboard, and is now
A Seaman, a grey headed Mariner.

Strange fits of passion I have known,
And I will dare to tell,
But in the lover's ear alone,
What once to me befel.

When she I loved, was strong and gay
And like a rose in June,
I to her cottage bent my way,
Beneath the evening moon.

Upon the moon I fixed my eye,
All over the wide lea;
My horse trudged on, and we drew nigh
Those paths so dear to me.

And now we reached the orchard plot,
And, as we climbed the hill,
Towards the roof of Lucy's cot
The moon descended still.

In one of those sweet dreams I slept,
Kind Nature's gentlest boon!
And, all the while, my eyes I kept
On the descending moon.

My horse moved on; hoof after hoof
He raised and never stopped:
When down behind the cottage roof
At once the planet dropped.

What fond and wayward thoughts will slide
Into a Lover's head—
'O mercy!' to myself I cried,
'If Lucy should be dead!'

SONG

She dwelt among th' untrodden ways
  Beside the springs of Dove,
A Maid whom there were none to praise
  And very few to love.

A Violet by a mossy stone
  Half-hidden from the Eye!
—Fair, as a star when only one
  Is shining in the sky!

She *lived* unknown, and few could know
  When Lucy ceased to be;
But she is in her Grave, and Oh!
  The difference to me.

A slumber did my spirit seal,
　　I had no human fears:
She seemed a thing that could not feel
　　The touch of earthly years.

No motion has she now, no force
　　She neither hears nor sees
Rolled round in earth's diurnal course
　　With rocks and stones and trees!

LUCY GRAY

Oft I had heard of Lucy Gray,
And when I crossed the Wild,
I chanced to see at break of day
The solitary Child.

No Mate, no comrade Lucy knew;
She dwelt on a wild Moor,
The sweetest Thing that ever grew
Beside a human door!

You yet may spy the Fawn at play,
The Hare upon the Green;
But the sweet face of Lucy Gray
Will never more be seen.

'To-night will be a stormy night,
You to the Town must go,
And take a lantern, Child, to light
Your Mother thro' the snow.'

'That, Father! will I gladly do;
'Tis scarcely afternoon—
The Minster-clock has just struck two,
And yonder is the Moon.'

At this the Father raised his hook
And snapped a faggot-band;
He plied his work, and Lucy took
The lantern in her hand.

Not blither is the mountain roe,
With many a wanton stroke
Her feet disperse, the powd'ry snow
That rises up like smoke.

The storm came on before its time,
She wandered up and down,
And many a hill did Lucy climb
But never reached the Town.

The wretched Parents all that night
Went shouting far and wide;
But there was neither sound nor sight
To serve them for a guide.

At day-break on a hill they stood
That overlooked the Moor;
And thence they saw the Bridge of Wood
A furlong from their door.

And now they homeward turned, and cried
'In Heaven we all shall meet!'
When in the snow the Mother spied
The print of Lucy's feet.

Then downward from the steep hill's edge
They tracked the footmarks small;
And through the broken hawthorn-hedge,
And by the long stone-wall;

And then an open field they crossed,
The marks were still the same;
They tracked them on, nor ever lost,
And to the Bridge they came.

They followed from the snowy bank
The footmarks, one by one,
Into the middle of the plank,
And further there were none.

Yet some maintain that to this day
She is a living Child,
That you may see sweet Lucy Gray
Upon the lonesome Wild.

O'er rough and smooth she trips along,
And never looks behind;
And sings a solitary song
That whistles in the wind.

A whirl-blast from behind the hill
Rushed o'er the wood with startling sound:
Then all at once the air was still,
And showers of hail-stones pattered round.
Where leafless Oaks towered high above,
I sate within an undergrove
Of tallest hollies, tall and green,
A fairer bower was never seen.
From year to year the spacious floor
With withered leaves is covered o'er,
You could not lay a hair between:
And all the year the bower is green.
But see! where'er the hailstones drop
The withered leaves all skip and hop,
There's not a breeze—no breath of air—
Yet here, and there, and every where
Along the floor, beneath the shade
By those embowering hollies made,
The leaves in myriads jump and spring,
As if with pipes and music rare
Some Robin Good-fellow were there,
And all those leaves, that jump and spring,
Were each a joyous, living thing.

Oh! grant me Heaven a heart at ease
That I may never cease to find,
Even in appearances like these
Enough to nourish and to stir my mind!

THE TWO APRIL MORNINGS

We walked along, while bright and red
Uprose the morning sun,
And Matthew stopped, he looked, and said,
'The will of God be done!'

A village Schoolmaster was he,
With hair of glittering grey;
As blithe a man as you could see
On a spring holiday.

And on that morning, through the grass,
And by the steaming rills,
We travelled merrily to pass
A day among the hills.

'Our work,' said I, 'was well begun;
Then, from thy breast what thought,
Beneath so beautiful a sun,
So sad a sigh has brought?'

A second time did Matthew stop,
And fixing still his eye
Upon the eastern mountain-top
To me he made reply.

Yon cloud with that long purple cleft
Brings fresh into my mind
A day like this which I have left
Full thirty years behind.

And on that slope of springing corn
The self-same crimson hue
Fell from the sky that April morn,
The same which now I view!

With rod and line my silent sport
I plied by Derwent's wave,
And, coming to the church, stopped short
Beside my Daughter's grave.

Nine summers had she scarcely seen
The pride of all the vale;
And then she sang!—she would have been
A very nightingale.

Six feet in earth my Emma lay,
And yet I loved her more,
For so it seemed, than till that day
I e'er had loved before.

And, turning from her grave, I met
Beside the church-yard Yew
A blooming Girl, whose hair was wet
With points of morning dew.

THE FOUNTAIN,
A Conversation.

We talked with open heart, and tongue
Affectionate and true,
A pair of Friends, though I was young,
And Matthew seventy-two.

We lay beneath a spreading oak,
Beside a mossy seat,
And from the turf a fountain broke,
And gurgled at our feet.

Now, Matthew, let us try to match
This water's pleasant tune
With some old Border-song, or catch
That suits a summer's noon.

Or of the Church-clock and the chimes
Sing here beneath the shade,
That half-mad thing of witty rhymes
Which you last April made!

In silence Matthew lay, and eyed
The spring beneath the tree;
And thus the dear old Man replied,
The grey-haired Man of glee.

'Down to the vale this water steers,
How merrily it goes!
'Twill murmur on a thousand years,
And flow as now it flows.

And here, on this delightful day,
I cannot chuse but think
How oft, a vigorous Man, I lay
Beside this Fountain's brink.

My eyes are dim with childish tears.
My heart is idly stirred,
For the same sound is in my ears,
Which in those days I heard.

Thus fares it still in our decay:
And yet the wiser mind
Mourns less for what age takes away
Than what it leaves behind.

The blackbird in the summer trees,
The lark upon the hill,
Let loose their carols when they please,
Are quiet when they will.

With Nature never do *they* wage
A foolish strife; they see
A happy youth, and their old age
Is beautiful and free:

But we are pressed by heavy laws,
And often, glad no more,
We wear a face of joy, because
We have been glad of yore.

If there is one who need bemoan
His kindred laid in earth,
The houshold hearts that were his own,
It is the man of mirth.

My days, my Friend, are almost gone,
My life has been approved,
And many love me, but by none
Am I enough beloved.'

'Now both himself and me he wrongs,
The man who thus complains!
I live and sing my idle songs
Upon these happy plains,

And, Matthew, for thy Children dead
I'll be a son to thee!'
At this he grasped his hands, and said,
'Alas! that cannot be.'

We rose up from the fountain-side,
And down the smooth descent
Of the green sheep-track did we glide,
And through the wood we went,

And, ere we came to Leonard's Rock,
He sang those witty rhymes
About the crazy old church-clock
And the bewildered chimes.

NUTTING

                    ——It seems a day,
(I speak of one from many singled out)
One of those heavenly days which cannot die,
When forth I sallied from our cottage-door,*
And with a wallet o'er my shoulder slung,
A nutting crook in hand, I turned my steps
Towards the distant woods, a Figure quaint,
Tricked out in proud disguise of Beggar's weeds
Put on for the occasion, by advice
And exhortation of my frugal Dame.
Motley accoutrement! of power to smile
At thorns, and brakes, and brambles, and, in truth,
More ragged than need was. Among the woods,
And o'er the pathless rocks, I forced my way
Until, at length, I came to one dear nook
Unvisited, where not a broken bough
Drooped with its withered leaves, ungracious sign
Of devastation, but the hazels rose
Tall and erect, with milk-white clusters hung,
A virgin scene!—A little while I stood,
Breathing with such suppression of the heart
As joy delights in; and with wise restraint
Voluptuous, fearless of a rival, eyed
The banquet, or beneath the trees I sate
Among the flowers, and with the flowers I played;
A temper known to those, who, after long
And weary expectation, have been blessed
With sudden happiness beyond all hope.—

* The house at which I was boarded during the time
I was at School.

—Perhaps it was a bower beneath whose leaves
The violets of five seasons re-appear
And fade, unseen by any human eye,
Where fairy water-breaks do murmur on
For ever, and I saw the sparkling foam,
And with my cheek on one of those green stones
That, fleeced with moss, beneath the shady trees,
Lay round me scattered like a flock of sheep,
I heard the murmur and the murmuring sound,
In that sweet mood when pleasure loves to pay
Tribute to ease, and, of its joy secure
The heart luxuriates with indifferent things,
Wasting its kindliness on stocks and stones,
And on the vacant air. Then up I rose,
And dragged to earth both branch and bough, with crash
And merciless ravage; and the shady nook
Of hazels, and the green and mossy bower
Deformed and sullied, patiently gave up
Their quiet being: and unless I now
Confound my present feelings with the past,
Even then, when, from the bower I turned away,
Exulting, rich beyond the wealth of kings
I felt a sense of pain when I beheld
The silent trees and the intruding sky.—

   Then, dearest Maiden! move along these shades
In gentleness of heart with gentle hand
Touch,—for there is a Spirit in the woods.

―――――

Three years she grew in sun and shower,
Then Nature said, 'A lovelier flower
On earth was never sown;
This Child I to myself will take,
She shall be mine, and I will make
A Lady of my own.

Myself will to my darling be
Both law and impulse, and with me
The Girl in rock and plain,
In earth and heaven, in glade and bower,
Shall feel an overseeing power
To kindle or restrain.

She shall be sportive as the fawn
That wild with glee across the lawn
Or up the mountain springs,
And hers shall be the breathing balm,
And hers the silence and the calm
Of mute insensate things.

The floating clouds their state shall lend
To her, for her the willow bend,
Nor shall she fail to see
Even in the motions of the storm
Grace that shall mould the Maiden's form
By silent sympathy.

The stars of midnight shall be dear
To her, and she shall lean her ear
In many a secret place
Where rivulets dance their wayward round,
And beauty born of murmuring sound
Shall pass into her face.

And vital feelings of delight
Shall rear her form to stately height,
Her virgin bosom swell,
Such thoughts to Lucy I will give
While she and I together live
Here in this happy dell.'

Thus Nature spake—The work was done—
How soon my Lucy's race was run!
She died and left to me
This heath, this calm and quiet scene,
The memory of what has been,
And never more will be.

THE OLD CUMBERLAND BEGGAR,

A Description.

The class of Beggars to which the old man here described belongs, will probably soon be extinct. It consisted of poor, and, mostly, old and infirm persons, who confined themselves to a stated round in their neighbourhood, and had certain fixed days, on which, at different houses, they regularly received charity; sometimes in money, but mostly in provisions.

I saw an aged Beggar in my walk,
And he was seated by the highway side
On a low structure of rude masonry
Built at the foot of a huge hill, that they
Who lead their horses down the steep rough road
May thence remount at ease. The aged man
Had placed his staff across the broad smooth stone
That overlays the pile, and from a bag
All white with flour the dole of village dames,
He drew his scraps and fragments, one by one,
And scanned them with a fixed and serious look
Of idle computation. In the sun,
Upon the second step of that small pile,
Surrounded by those wild unpeopled hills,
He sate, and eat his food in solitude;
And ever, scattered from his palsied hand,
That still attempting to prevent the waste,
Was baffled still, the crumbs in little showers
Fell on the ground, and the small mountain birds,
Not venturing yet to peck their destined meal,
Approached within the length of half his staff.

Him from my childhood have I known, and then
He was so old, he seems not older now;
He travels on, a solitary man,
So helpless in appearance, that for him
The sauntering horseman-traveller does not throw
With careless hand his alms upon the ground,
But stops, that he may safely lodge the coin
Within the old Man's hat; nor quits him so,
But still, when he has given his horse the rein
Towards the aged Beggar turns a look,
Sidelong and half-reverted. She who tends
The toll-gate, when in summer at her door
She turns her wheel, if on the road she sees
The aged Beggar coming, quits her work,
And lifts the latch for him that he may pass.
The Post-boy when his rattling wheels o'ertake
The aged Beggar, in the woody lane,
Shouts to him from behind, and, if perchance
The old Man does not change his course, the Boy
Turns with less noisy wheels to the road-side,
And passes gently by, without a curse
Upon his lips, or anger at his heart.
He travels on, a solitary Man,
His age has no companion. On the ground
His eyes are turned, and, as he moves along,
They move along the ground; and evermore,
Instead of common and habitual sight
Of fields with rural works, of hill and dale,
And the blue sky, one little span of earth
Is all his prospect. Thus, from day to day,
Bowbent, his eyes for ever on the ground,

He plies his weary journey, seeing still,
And never knowing that he sees, some straw,
Some scattered leaf, or marks which, in one track,
The nails of cart or chariot wheel have left
Impressed on the white road, in the same line,
At distance still the same. Poor Traveller!
His staff trails with him, scarcely do his feet
Disturb the summer dust, he is so still
In look and motion that the cottage curs,
Ere he have passed the door, will turn away
Weary of barking at him. Boys and girls,
The vacant and the busy, maids and youths,
And urchins newly breeched all pass him by:
Him even the slow-paced waggon leaves behind.

But deem not this man useless.—Statesmen! ye
Who are so restless in your wisdom, ye
Who have a broom still ready in your hands
To rid the world of nuisances; ye proud,
Heart-swoln, while in your pride ye contemplate
Your talents, power, and wisdom, deem him not
A burthen of the earth. 'Tis Nature's law
That none, the meanest of created things,
Or forms created the most vile and brute,
The dullest or most noxious, should exist
Divorced from good, a spirit and pulse of good,
A life and soul to every mode of being
Inseparably linked. While thus he creeps
From door to door, the Villagers in him
Behold a record which together binds
Past deeds and offices of charity
Else unremembered, and so keeps alive

The kindly mood in hearts which lapse of years,
And that half-wisdom half-experience gives
Make slow to feel, and by sure steps resign
To selfishness and cold oblivious cares.
Among the farms and solitary huts
Hamlets, and thinly-scattered villages,
Where'er the aged Beggar takes his rounds,
The mild necessity of use compels
To acts of love; and habit does the work
Of reason, yet prepares that after joy
Which reason cherishes. And thus the soul,
By that sweet taste of pleasure unpursued
Doth find itself insensibly disposed
To virtue and true goodness. Some there are,
By their good works exalted, lofty minds
And meditative, authors of delight
And happiness, which to the end of time
Will live, and spread, and kindle; minds like these,
In childhood, from this solitary being,
This helpless wanderer, haply have received
(A thing more precious far than all that books
Or the solicitudes of love can do!)
That first mild touch of sympathy and thought,
In which they found their kindred with a world
Where want and sorrow were. The easy man
Who sits at his own door, and like the pear
Which overhangs his head from the green wall,
Feeds in the sunshine; the robust and young,
The prosperous and unthinking, they who live
Sheltered, and flourish in a little grove
Of their own kindred, all behold in him
A silent monitor, which on their minds

Must needs impress a transitory thought
Of self-congratulation, to the heart
Of each recalling his peculiar boons,
His charters and exemptions; and perchance,
Though he to no one give the fortitude
And circumspection needful to preserve
His present blessings, and to husband up
The respite of the season, he, at least,
And 'tis no vulgar service, makes them felt.

Yet further.——Many, I believe, there are
Who live a life of virtuous decency,
Men who can hear the Decalogue and feel
No self-reproach, who of the moral law
Established in the land where they abide
Are strict observers, and not negligent,
Meanwhile, in any tenderness of heart
Or act of love to those with whom they dwell,
Their kindred, and the children of their blood.
Praise be to such, and to their slumbers peace!
—But of the poor man ask, the abject poor,
Go and demand of him, if there be here,
In this cold abstinence from evil deeds,
And these inevitable charities,
Wherewith to satisfy the human soul.
No—man is dear to man: the poorest poor
Long for some moments in a weary life
When they can know and feel that they have been
Themselves the fathers and the dealers out
Of some small blessings, have been kind to such
As needed kindness, for this single cause,
That we have all of us one human heart.

—Such pleasure is to one kind Being known
My Neighbour, when with punctual care, each week
Duly as Friday comes, though pressed herself
By her own wants, she from her chest of meal
Takes one unsparing handful for the scrip
Of this old Mendicant, and, from her door
Returning with exhilarated heart,
Sits by her fire and builds her hope in heav'n.

Then let him pass, a blessing on his head!
And while, in that vast solitude to which
The tide of things has led him, he appears
To breathe and live but for himself alone,
Unblamed, uninjured, let him bear about
The good which the benignant law of heaven
Has hung around him, and, while life is his,
Still let him prompt the unlettered Villagers
To tender offices and pensive thoughts.
Then let him pass, a blessing on his head!
And, long as he can wander, let him breathe
The freshness of the vallies, let his blood
Struggle with frosty air and winter snows,
And let the chartered wind that sweeps the heath
Beat his grey locks against his withered face.
Reverence the hope whose vital anxiousness
Gives the last human interest to his heart.
May never House, misnamed of industry,
Make him a captive; for that pent-up din,
Those life-consuming sounds that clog the air,
Be his the natural silence of old age.
Let him be free of mountain solitudes,
And have around him, whether heard or not,

The pleasant melody of woodland birds.
Few are his pleasures; if his eyes, which now
Have been so long familiar with the earth,
No more behold the horizontal sun
Rising or setting, let the light at least
Find a free entrance to their languid orbs.
And let him, *where* and *when* he will, sit down
Beneath the trees, or on a grassy bank
Of high-way side, and with the little birds
Share his chance-gathered meal, and, finally,
As in the eye of Nature he has lived,
So in the eye of Nature let him die.

MICHAEL,

A Pastoral Poem.

If from the public way you turn your steps
Up the tumultuous brook of Green-head Gill,
You will suppose that with an upright path
Your feet must struggle; in such bold ascent
The pastoral Mountains front you, face to face.
But, courage! for beside that boisterous Brook
The mountains have all opened out themselves,
And made a hidden valley of their own.
No habitation there is seen; but such
As journey thither find themselves alone
With a few sheep, with rocks and stones, and kites
That overhead are sailing in the sky.
It is in truth an utter solitude,
Nor should I have made mention of this Dell
But for one object which you might pass by,
Might see and notice not. Beside the brook
There is a straggling heap of unhewn stones!
And to that place a story appertains,
Which, though it be ungarnished with events,
Is not unfit, I deem, for the fire-side,
Or for the summer shade. It was the first,
The earliest of those tales that spake to me
Of Shepherds, dwellers in the vallies, men
Whom I already loved, not verily
For their own sakes, but for the fields and hills
Where was their occupation and abode.
And hence this Tale, while I was yet a boy
Careless of books, yet having felt the power
Of Nature, by the gentle agency

Of natural objects led me on to feel
For passions that were not my own, and think
At random and imperfectly indeed
On man; the heart of man and human life.
Therefore, although it be a history
Homely and rude, I will relate the same
For the delight of a few natural hearts,
And with yet fonder feeling, for the sake
Of youthful Poets, who among these Hills
Will be my second self when I am gone.

Upon the Forest-side in Grasmere Vale
There dwelt a Shepherd, Michael was his name,
An old man, stout of heart, and strong of limb.
His bodily frame had been from youth to age
Of an unusual strength: his mind was keen
Intense and frugal, apt for all affairs,
And in his Shepherd's calling he was prompt
And watchful more than ordinary men.
Hence he had learned the meaning of all winds,
Of blasts of every tone, and often-times
When others heeded not, He heard the South
Make subterraneous music, like the noise
Of Bagpipers on distant Highland hills;
The Shepherd, at such warning, of his flock
Bethought him, and he to himself would say
The winds are now devising work for me!
And truly at all times the storm, that drives
The Traveller to a shelter, summoned him
Up to the mountains: he had been alone
Amid the heart of many thousand mists

That came to him and left him on the heights.
So lived he till his eightieth year was passed.

And grossly that man errs, who should suppose
That the green Valleys, and the Streams and Rocks
Were things indifferent to the Shepherd's thoughts.
Fields, where with chearful spirits he had breathed
The common air; the hills, which he so oft
Had climbed with vigorous steps; which had impressed
So many incidents upon his mind
Of hardship, skill or courage, joy or fear;
Which like a book preserved the memory
Of the dumb animals, whom he had saved,
Had fed or sheltered, linking to such acts,
So grateful in themselves, the certainty
Of honorable gains; these fields, these hills
Which were his living Being, even more
Than his own Blood—what could they less? had laid
Strong hold on his affections, were to him
A pleasurable feeling of blind love,
The pleasure which there is in life itself.

He had not passed his days in singleness.
He had a Wife, a comely Matron, old
Though younger than himself full twenty years.
She was a woman of a stirring life
Whose heart was in her house: two wheels she had
Of antique form, this large for spinning wool,
That small for flax, and if one wheel had rest,
It was because the other was at work.
The Pair had but one Inmate in their house,

An only Child, who had been born to them
When Michael telling o'er his years began
To deem that he was old, in Shepherd's phrase,
With one foot in the grave. This only son,
With two brave sheep dogs tried in many a storm,
The one of an inestimable worth,
Made all their Household. I may truly say,
That they were as a proverb in the vale
For endless industry. When day was gone,
And from their occupations out of doors
The Son and Father were come home, even then
Their labour did not cease, unless when all
Turned to their cleanly supper-board, and there
Each with a mess of pottage and skimmed milk,
Sate round their basket piled with oaten cakes,
And their plain home-made cheese. Yet when their meal
Was ended, LUKE (for so the Son was named)
And his old Father, both betook themselves
To such convenient work, as might employ
Their hands by the fire-side; perhaps to card
Wool for the House-wife's spindle, or repair
Some injury done to sickle, flail, or scythe,
Or other implement of house or field.

Down from the ceiling by the chimney's edge,
Which in our ancient uncouth country style
Did with a huge projection overbrow
Large space beneath, as duly as the light
Of day grew dim, the House-wife hung a lamp;
An aged utensil, which had performed
Service beyond all others of its kind.
Early at evening did it burn and late,

Surviving Comrade of uncounted Hours
Which going by from year to year had found
And left the Couple neither gay perhaps
Nor chearful, yet with objects and with hopes
Living a life of eager industry.
And now, when LUKE was in his eighteenth year,
There by the light of this old lamp they sate,
Father and Son, while late into the night
The House-wife plied her own peculiar work,
Making the cottage thro' the silent hours
Murmur as with the sound of summer flies.
Not with a waste of words, but for the sake
Of pleasure, which I know that I shall give
To many living now, I of this Lamp
Speak thus minutely: for there are no few
Whose memories will bear witness to my tale.
The Light was famous in its neighbourhood,
And was a public Symbol of the life,
The thrifty Pair had lived. For, as it chanced,
Their Cottage on a plot of rising ground
Stood single, with large prospect North and South,
High into Easedale, up to Dunmal-Raise,
And Westward to the village near the Lake.
And from this constant light so regular
And so far seen, the House itself by all
Who dwelt within the limits of the vale,
Both old and young, was named The Evening Star.

Thus living on through such a length of years,
The Shepherd, if he loved himself, must needs
Have loved his Help-mate; but to Michael's heart
This Son of his old age was yet more dear—

Effect which might perhaps have been produced
By that instinctive tenderness, the same
Blind Spirit, which is in the blood of all,
Or that a child, more than all other gifts,
Brings hope with it, and forward-looking thoughts,
And stirrings of inquietude, when they
By tendency of nature needs must fail.
From such, and other causes, to the thoughts
Of the old Man his only Son was now
The dearest object that he knew on earth.
Exceeding was the love he bare to him,
His Heart and his Heart's joy! For oftentimes
Old Michael, while he was a babe in arms,
Had done him female service, not alone
For dalliance and delight, as is the use
Of Fathers, but with patient mind enforced
To acts of tenderness; and he had rocked
His cradle with a woman's gentle hand.

And in a later time, ere yet the Boy
Had put on Boy's attire, did Michael love,
Albeit of a stern unbending mind,
To have the young one in his sight, when he
Had work by his own door, or when he sate
With sheep before him on his Shepherd's stool,
Beneath that large old Oak, which near their door
Stood, and from its enormous breadth of shade
Chosen for the Shearer's covert from the sun,
Thence in our rustic dialect was called
The CLIPPING TREE,* a name which yet it bears.

* Clipping is the word used in the North of England for shearing.

There, while they two were sitting in the shade,
With others round them, earnest all and blithe,
Would Michael exercise his heart with looks
Of fond correction and reproof bestowed
Upon the child, if he disturbed the sheep
By catching at their legs, or with his shouts
Scared them, while they lay still beneath the shears.

And when by Heaven's good grace the Boy grew up
A healthy Lad, and carried in his cheek
Two steady roses that were five years old,
Then Michael from a winter coppice cut
With his own hand a sapling, which he hooped
With iron, making it throughout in all
Due requisites a perfect Shepherd's Staff,
And gave it to the Boy; wherewith equipped
He as a Watchman oftentimes was placed
At gate or gap, to stem or turn the flock,
And to his office prematurely called
There stood the urchin, as you will divine,
Something between a hindrance and a help,
And for this cause not always, I believe,
Receiving from his Father hire of praise.
Though nought was left undone, which staff or voice,
Or looks, or threatening gestures could perform.
    But soon as Luke, full ten years old, could stand
Against the mountain blasts, and to the heights,
Not fearing toil, nor length of weary ways,
He with his Father daily went, and they
Were as companions, why should I relate
That objects which the Shepherd loved before
Were dearer now? that from the Boy there came

Feelings and emanations, things which were
Light to the sun and music to the wind;
And that the Old Man's heart seemed born again.
   Thus in his Father's sight the Boy grew up:
And now when he had reached his eighteenth year,
He was his comfort and his daily hope.

While this good household thus were living on
From day to day, to Michael's ear there came
Distressful tidings. Long before the time
Of which I speak, the Shepherd had been bound
In surety for his Brother's Son, a man
Of an industrious life, and ample means,
But unforseen misfortunes suddenly
Had pressed upon him, and old Michael now
Was summoned to discharge the forfeiture,
A grievous penalty, but little less
Than half his substance. This un-looked for claim
At the first hearing, for a moment took
More hope out of his life than he supposed
That any old man ever could have lost.
As soon as he had gathered so much strength
That he could look his trouble in the face,
It seemed that his sole refuge was to sell
A portion of his patrimonial fields.
Such was his first resolve; he thought again,
And his heart failed him. 'Isabel,' said he,
Two evenings after he had heard the news,
'I have been toiling more than seventy years,
And in the open sun-shine of God's love
Have we all lived, yet if these fields of ours
Should pass into a Stranger's hand, I think

That I could not lie quiet in my grave.
Our lot is a hard lot; the Sun itself
Has scarcely been more diligent than I,
And I have lived to be a fool at last
To my own family. An evil Man
That was, and made an evil choice, if he
Were false to us; and if he were not false,
There are ten thousand to whom loss like this
Had been no sorrow. I forgive him—but
'Twere better to be dumb than to talk thus.

When I began, my purpose was to speak
Of remedies and of a chearful hope.
Our Luke shall leave us, Isabel; the land
Shall not go from us, and it shall be free,
He shall possess it, free as is the wind
That passes over it. We have, thou knowest,
Another Kinsman, he will be our friend
In this distress. He is a prosperous man,
Thriving in trade, and Luke to him shall go,
And with his Kinsman's help and his own thrift,
He quickly will repair this loss, and then
May come again to us. If here he stay,
What can be done? Where every one is poor
What can be gained?' At this, the old man paused,
And Isabel sate silent, for her mind
Was busy, looking back into past times.
There's Richard Bateman, thought she to herself,
He was a parish-boy—at the church-door
They made a gathering for him, shillings, pence,
And halfpennies, wherewith the Neighbours bought
A Basket, which they filled with Pedlar's wares,
And with this Basket on his arm, the Lad

Went up to London, found a Master there,
Who out of many chose the trusty Boy
To go and overlook his merchandise
Beyond the seas, where he grew wond'rous rich,
And left estates and monies to the poor,
And at his birth-place built a Chapel, floored
With Marble, which he sent from foreign lands.
These thoughts, and many others of like sort,
Passed quickly thro' the mind of Isabel,
And her face brightened. The Old Man was glad,
And thus resumed. 'Well! Isabel, this scheme
These two days has been meat and drink to me.
Far more than we have lost is left us yet.
—We have enough—I wish indeed that I
Were younger, but this hope is a good hope.
—Make ready Luke's best garments, of the best
Buy for him more, and let us send him forth
To-morrow, or the next day, or to-night:
—If he could go, the Boy should go to-night.'
Here Michael ceased, and to the fields went forth
With a light heart. The House-wife for five days
Was restless morn and night, and all day long
Wrought on with her best fingers to prepare
Things needful for the journey of her Son.
But Isabel was glad when Sunday came
To stop her in her work; for, when she lay
By Michael's side, she for the last two nights
Heard him, how he was troubled in his sleep:
And when they rose at morning she could see
That all his hopes were gone. That day at noon
She said to Luke, while they two by themselves
Were sitting at the door, 'Thou must not go,

We have no other Child but thee to lose,
None to remember—do not go away,
For if thou leave thy Father he will die.'
The Lad made answer with a jocund voice,
And Isabel, when she had told her fears,
Recovered heart. That evening her best fare
Did she bring forth, and all together sate
Like happy people round a Christmas fire.

Next morning Isabel resumed her work,
And all the ensuing week the house appeared
As cheerful as a grove in Spring: at length
The expected letter from their Kinsman came,
With kind assurances that he would do
His utmost for the welfare of the Boy,
To which requests were added that forthwith
He might be sent to him. Ten times or more
The letter was read over; Isabel
Went forth to shew it to the neighbours round:
Nor was there at that time on English Land
A prouder heart than Luke's. When Isabel
Had to her house returned, the Old Man said
'He shall depart to-morrow.' To this word
The House-wife answered, talking much of things
Which, if at such short notice he should go,
Would surely be forgotten. But at length
She gave consent, and Michael was at ease.

Near the tumultuous brook of Green-head Gill,
In that deep Valley, Michael had designed
To build a Sheep-fold, and, before he heard
The tidings of his melancholy loss,

For this same purpose he had gathered up
A heap of stones, which close to the brook side
Lay thrown together, ready for the work.
With Luke that evening thitherward he walked;
And soon as they had reached the place he stopped
And thus the Old Man spake to him. 'My Son,
To-morrow thou wilt leave me; with full heart
I look upon thee, for thou art the same
That wert a promise to me ere thy birth.
And all thy life hast been my daily joy.
I will relate to thee some little part
Of our two histories; 'twill do thee good
When thou art from me, even if I should speak
Of things thou canst not know of.—After thou
First cam'st into the world, as it befalls
To new-born infants, thou didst sleep away
Two days, and blessings from thy Father's tongue
Then fell upon thee. Day by day passed on,
And still I loved thee with encreasing love.
Never to living ear came sweeter sounds
Than when I heard thee by our own fire-side
First uttering without words a natural tune,
When thou, a feeding babe, didst in thy joy
Sing at thy Mother's breast. Month followed month,
And in the open fields my life was passed
And in the mountains, else I think that thou
Hadst been brought up upon thy father's knees.
—But we were playmates, Luke; among these hills,
As well thou know'st, in us the old and young
Have played together, nor with me didst thou
Lack any pleasure which a boy can know.'
Luke had a manly heart; but at these words

He sobbed aloud; the Old Man grasped his hand,
And said, 'Nay do not take it so—I see
That these are things of which I need not speak.
—Even to the utmost I have been to thee
A kind and a good Father: and herein
I but repay a gift which I myself
Received at others hands, for, though now old
Beyond the common life of man, I still
Remember them who loved me in my youth.
Both of them sleep together: here they lived
As all their Forefathers had done, and when
At length their time was come, they were not loth
To give their bodies to the family mold.
I wished that thou should'st live the life they lived.
But 'tis a long time to look back, my Son,
And see so little gain from sixty years.
These fields were burthened when they came to me;
'Till I was forty years of age, not more
Than half of my inheritance was mine.
I toiled and toiled; God blessed me in my work,
And 'till these three weeks past the land was free.
—It looks as if it never could endure
Another Master. Heaven forgive me, Luke,
If I judge ill for thee, but it seems good
That thou should'st go.' At this the Old Man paused,
Then, pointing to the Stones near which they stood,
Thus, after a short silence, he resumed:
'This was a work for us, and now, my Son,
It is a work for me. But, lay one Stone—
Here, lay it for me, Luke, with thine own hands.
I for the purpose brought thee to this place.
Nay, Boy, be of good hope:—we both may live

To see a better day. At eighty-four
I still am strong and stout;—do thou thy part,
I will do mine.—I will begin again
With many tasks that were resigned to thee;
Up to the heights, and in among the storms,
Will I without thee go again, and do
All works which I was wont to do alone,
Before I knew thy face.—Heaven bless thee, Boy!
Thy heart these two weeks has been beating fast
With many hopes—it should be so—yes—yes—
I knew that thou could'st never have a wish
To leave me, Luke, thou hast been bound to me
Only by links of love, when thou art gone
What will be left to us!—But, I forget
My purposes. Lay now the corner-stone,
As I requested, and hereafter, Luke,
When thou art gone away, should evil men
Be thy companions, let this Sheep-fold be
Thy anchor and thy shield; amid all fear
And all temptation, let it be to thee
An emblem of the life thy Fathers lived,
Who, being innocent, did for that cause
Bestir them in good deeds. Now, fare thee well—
When thou return'st, thou in this place wilt see
A work which is not here, a covenant
'Twill be between us—but whatever fate
Befall thee, I shall love thee to the last,
And bear thy memory with me to the grave.'

The Shepherd ended here; and Luke stooped down,
And as his Father had requested, laid
The first stone of the Sheep-fold; at the sight

The Old Man's grief broke from him, to his heart
He pressed his Son, he kissed him and wept;
And to the House together they returned.

Next morning, as had been resolved, the Boy
Began his journey, and when he had reached
The public Way, he put on a bold face;
And all the Neighbours as he passed their doors
Came forth, with wishes and with farewell prayers,
That followed him 'till he was out of sight.
A good report did from their Kinsman come,
Of Luke and his well-doing; and the Boy
Wrote loving letters, full of wond'rous news,
Which, as the House-wife phrased it, were throughout
The prettiest letters that were ever seen.
Both parents read them with rejoicing hearts.
So, many months passed on: and once again
The Shepherd went about his daily work
With confident and cheerful thoughts; and now
Sometimes when he could find a leisure hour
He to that valley took his way, and there
Wrought at the Sheep-fold. Meantime Luke began
To slacken in his duty, and at length
He in the dissolute city gave himself
To evil courses: ignominy and shame
Fell on him, so that he was driven at last
To seek a hiding-place beyond the seas.

There is a comfort in the strength of love;
'Twill make a thing endurable, which else
Would break the heart:—Old Michael found it so.
I have conversed with more than one who well

Remember the Old Man, and what he was
Years after he had heard this heavy news.
His bodily frame had been from youth to age
Of an unusual strength. Among the rocks
He went, and still looked up upon the sun,
And listened to the wind; and as before
Performed all kinds of labour for his Sheep,
And for the land his small inheritance.
And to that hollow Dell from time to time
Did he repair, to build the Fold of which
His flock had need. 'Tis not forgotten yet
The pity which was then in every heart
For the Old Man—and 'tis believed by all
That many and many a day he thither went,
And never lifted up a single stone.
There, by the Sheep-fold, sometimes was he seen
Sitting alone, with that his faithful Dog,
Then old, beside him, lying at his feet.
The length of full seven years from time to time
He at the building of this Sheep-fold wrought,
And left the work unfinished when he died.

Three years, or little more, did Isabel,
Survive her Husband: at her death the estate
Was sold, and went into a Stranger's hand.
The Cottage which was named The Evening Star
Is gone, the ploughshare has been through the ground
On which it stood; great changes have been wrought
In all the neighbourhood, yet the Oak is left
That grew beside their Door; and the remains
Of the unfinished Sheep-fold may be seen
Beside the boisterous brook of Green-head Gill.

POEMS, IN TWO VOLUMES

(1807)

POEMS,

IN

TWO VOLUMES,

BY

WILLIAM WORDSWORTH,

AUTHOR OF

THE LYRICAL BALLADS.

Posterius graviore sono tibi Musa loquetur
Nostra: dabunt cum securos mihi tempora fructus.

VOL. I.

LONDON:

PRINTED FOR LONGMAN, HURST, REES, AND ORME,
PATERNOSTER-ROW.

1807.

TO H.C.,
SIX YEARS OLD.

O Thou! whose fancies from afar are brought;
Who of thy words dost make a mock apparel,
And fittest to unutterable thought
The breeze-like motion and the self-born carol;
Thou Faery Voyager! that dost float
In such clear water, that thy Boat
May rather seem
To brood on air than on an earthly stream;
Suspended in a stream as clear as sky,
Where earth and heaven do make one imagery;
O blessed Vision! happy Child!
That art so exquisitely wild,
I think of thee with many fears
For what may be thy lot in future years.

I thought of times when Pain might be thy guest,
Lord of thy house and hospitality;
And grief, uneasy Lover! never rest
But when she sate within the touch of thee.
Oh! too industrious folly!
Oh! vain and causeless melancholy!
Nature will either end thee quite;
Or, lengthening out thy season of delight,
Preserve for thee, by individual right,
A young Lamb's heart among the full-grown flocks.
What hast Thou to do with sorrow,
Or the injuries of tomorrow?
Thou art a Dew-drop, which the morn brings forth,
Not doomed to jostle with unkindly shocks;

Or to be trailed along the soiling earth;
A Gem that glitters while it lives,
And no forewarning gives;
But, at the touch of wrong, without a strife
Slips in a moment out of life.

I travelled among unknown Men,
    In Lands beyond the Sea;
Nor England! did I know till then
    What love I bore to thee.

'Tis past, that melancholy dream!
    Nor will I quit thy shore
A second time; for still I seem
    To love thee more and more.

Among thy mountains did I feel
    The joy of my desire;
And She I cherished turned her wheel
    Beside an English fire.

Thy mornings shewed—thy nights concealed
    The bowers where Lucy played;
And thine is, too, the last green field
    Which Lucy's eyes surveyed!

ODE TO DUTY

Stern Daughter of the Voice of God!
O Duty! if that name thou love
Who art a Light to guide, a Rod
To check the erring, and reprove;
Thou who art victory and law
When empty terrors overawe;
From vain temptations dost set free;
From strife and from despair; a glorious ministry.

There are who ask not if thine eye
Be on them; who, in love and truth,
Where no misgiving is, rely
Upon the genial sense of youth:
Glad Hearts! without reproach or blot;
Who do thy work, and know it not:
May joy be theirs while life shall last!
And Thou, if they should totter, teach them to stand fast!

Serene will be our days and bright,
And happy will our nature be,
When love is an unerring light,
And joy its own security.
And blessed are they who in the main
This faith, even now, do entertain:
Live in the spirit of this creed;
Yet find that other strength, according to their need.

I, loving freedom, and untried;
No sport of every random gust,
Yet being to myself a guide,
Too blindly have reposed my trust:
Resolved that nothing e'er should press
Upon my present happiness,
I shoved unwelcome tasks away;
But thee I now would serve more strictly, if I may.

Through no disturbance of my soul,
Or strong compunction in me wrought,
I supplicate for thy controul;
But in the quietness of thought:
Me this unchartered freedom tires;
I feel the weight of chance desires:
My hopes no more must change their name,
I long for a repose which ever is the same.

Yet not the less would I throughout
Still act according to the voice
Of my own wish; and feel past doubt
That my submissiveness was choice:
Not seeking in the school of pride
For 'precepts over dignified,'
Denial and restraint I prize
No farther than they breed a second Will more wise.

Stern Lawgiver! yet thou dost wear
The Godhead's most benignant grace;
Nor know we any thing so fair
As is the smile upon thy face;
Flowers laugh before thee on their beds;
And Fragrance in thy footing treads;
Thou dost preserve the Stars from wrong;
And the most ancient Heavens through Thee are
  fresh and strong.

To humbler functions, awful Power!
I call thee: I myself commend
Unto thy guidance from this hour;
Oh! let my weakness have an end!
Give unto me, made lowly wise,
The spirit of self-sacrifice;
The confidence of reason give;
And in the light of truth thy Bondman let me live!

RESOLUTION AND INDEPENDENCE

There was a roaring in the wind all night;
The rain came heavily and fell in floods;
But now the sun is rising calm and bright;
The birds are singing in the distant woods;
Over his own sweet voice the Stock-dove broods;
The Jay makes answer as the Magpie chatters;
And all the air is filled with pleasant noise of waters.

All things that love the sun are out of doors;
The sky rejoices in the morning's birth;
The grass is bright with rain-drops; on the moors
The Hare is running races in her mirth;
And with her feet she from the plashy earth
Raises a mist; which, glittering in the sun,
Runs with her all the way, wherever she doth run.

I was a Traveller then upon the moor;
I saw the Hare that raced about with joy;
I heard the woods, and distant waters, roar;
Or heard them not, as happy as a Boy:
The pleasant season did my heart employ:
My old remembrances went from me wholly;
And all the ways of men, so vain and melancholy.

But, as it sometimes chanceth, from the might
Of joy in minds that can no farther go,
As high as we have mounted in delight
In our dejection do we sink as low,
To me that morning did it happen so;
And fears, and fancies, thick upon me came;
Dim sadness, and blind thoughts I knew not nor could name.

I heard the Sky-lark singing in the sky;
And I bethought me of the playful Hare:
Even such a happy Child of earth am I;
Even as these blissful Creatures do I fare;
Far from the world I walk, and from all care;
But there may come another day to me,
Solitude, pain of heart, distress, and poverty.

My whole life I have lived in pleasant thought,
As if life's business were a summer mood;
As if all needful things would come unsought
To genial faith, still rich in genial good;
But how can He expect that others should
Build for him, sow for him, and at his call
Love him, who for himself will take no heed at all?

I thought of Chatterton, the marvellous Boy,
The sleepless Soul that perished in its pride;
Of Him who walked in glory and in joy
Behind his plough, upon the mountain-side:
By our own spirits are we deified;
We Poets in our youth begin in gladness;
But thereof comes in the end despondency and madness.

Now, whether it were by peculiar grace,
A leading from above, a something given,
Yet it befel, that, in this lonely place,
When up and down my fancy thus was driven,
And I with these untoward thoughts had striven,
I saw a Man before me unawares:
The oldest Man he seemed that ever wore grey hairs.

My course I stopped as soon as I espied
The Old Man in that naked wilderness:
Close by a Pond, upon the further side,
He stood alone: a minute's space I guess
I watched him, he continuing motionless:
To the Pool's further margin then I drew;
He being all the while before me full in view.

As a huge Stone is sometimes seen to lie
Couched on the bald top of an eminence;
Wonder to all who do the same espy
By what means it could thither come, and whence;
So that it seems a thing endued with sense:
Like a Sea-beast crawled forth, which on a shelf
Of rock or sand reposeth, there to sun itself.

Such seemed this Man, not all alive nor dead,
Nor all asleep; in his extreme old age:
His body was bent double, feet and head
Coming together in their pilgrimage;
As if some dire constraint of pain, or rage
Of sickness felt by him in times long past,
A more than human weight upon his frame had cast.

Himself he propped, his body, limbs, and face,
Upon a long grey Staff of shaven wood:
And, still as I drew near with gentle pace,
Beside the little pond or moorish flood
Motionless as a Cloud the Old Man stood;
That heareth not the loud winds when they call;
And moveth altogether, if it move at all.

At length, himself unsettling, he the Pond
Stirred with his Staff, and fixedly did look
Upon the muddy water, which he conned,
As if he had been reading in a book:
And now such freedom as I could I took;
And, drawing to his side, to him did say,
'This morning gives us promise of a glorious day.'

A gentle answer did the Old Man make,
In courteous speech which forth he slowly drew:
And him with further words I thus bespake,
'What kind of work is that which you pursue?
This is a lonesome place for one like you.'
He answered me with pleasure and surprize;
And there was, while he spake, a fire about his eyes.

His words came feebly, from a feeble chest,
Yet each in solemn order followed each,
With something of a lofty utterance drest;
Choice word, and measured phrase; above the reach
Of ordinary men; a stately speech!
Such as grave Livers do in Scotland use,
Religious men, who give to God and Man their dues.

He told me that he to this pond had come
To gather Leeches, being old and poor:
Employment hazardous and wearisome!
And he had many hardships to endure:
From Pond to Pond he roamed, from moor to moor,
Housing, with God's good help, by choice or chance:
And in this way he gained an honest maintenance.

The Old Man still stood talking by my side;
But now his voice to me was like a stream
Scarce heard; nor word from word could I divide;
And the whole Body of the man did seem
Like one whom I had met with in a dream;
Or like a Man from some far region sent;
To give me human strength, and strong admonishment.

My former thoughts returned: the fear that kills;
The hope that is unwilling to be fed;
Cold, pain, and labour, and all fleshly ills;
And mighty Poets in their misery dead.
And now, not knowing what the Old Man had said,
My question eagerly did I renew,
'How is it that you live, and what is it you do?'

He with a smile did then his words repeat;
And said, that, gathering Leeches, far and wide
He travelled; stirring thus about his feet
The waters of the Ponds where they abide.
'Once I could meet with them on every side;
But they have dwindled long by slow decay;
Yet still I persevere, and find them where I may.'

While he was talking thus, the lonely place,
The Old Man's shape, and speech, all troubled me:
In my mind's eye I seemed to see him pace
About the weary moors continually,
Wandering about alone and silently.
While I these thoughts within myself pursued,
He, having made a pause, the same discourse renewed.

And soon with this he other matter blended,
Chearfully uttered, with demeanour kind,
But stately in the main; and, when he ended,
I could have laughed myself to scorn, to find
In that decrepit Man so firm a mind.
'God', said I, 'be my help and stay secure;
I'll think of the Leech-gatherer on the lonely moor.'

Nuns fret not at their Convent's narrow room;
And Hermits are contented with their Cells;
And Students with their pensive Citadels:
Maids at the Wheel, the Weaver at his Loom,
Sit blithe and happy; Bees that soar for bloom,
High as the highest Peak of Furness Fells,
Will murmur by the hour in Foxglove bells:
In truth, the prison, unto which we doom
Ourselves, no prison is: and hence to me,
In sundry moods, 'twas pastime to be bound
Within the Sonnet's scanty plot of ground:
Pleased if some Souls (for such there needs must be)
Who have felt the weight of too much liberty,
Should find short solace there, as I have found.

With Ships the sea was sprinkled far and nigh,
Like stars in heaven, and joyously it showed;
Some lying fast at anchor in the road,
Some veering up and down, one knew not why.
A goodly Vessel did I then espy
Come like a Giant from a haven broad;
And lustily along the Bay she strode,
Her tackling rich, and of apparel high.
This Ship was nought to me, nor I to her,
Yet I pursued her with a Lover's look;
This Ship to all the rest did I prefer:
When will she turn, and whither? She will brook
No tarrying; where she comes the winds must stir:
On went She, and due north her journey took.

COMPOSED UPON WESTMINSTER BRIDGE,
SEPT. 3, 1803.

Earth has not any thing to shew more fair:
Dull would he be of soul who could pass by
A sight so touching in it's majesty:
This City now doth like a garment wear
The beauty of the morning; silent, bare,
Ships, towers, domes, theatres, and temples lie
Open unto the fields, and to the sky;
All bright and glittering in the smokeless air.
Never did sun more beautifully steep
In his first splendor valley, rock, or hill;
Ne'er saw I, never felt, a calm so deep!
The river glideth at his own sweet will:
Dear God! the very houses seem asleep;
And all that mighty heart is lying still!

The world is too much with us; late and soon,
Getting and spending, we lay waste our powers:
Little we see in nature that is ours;
We have given our hearts away, a sordid boon!
This Sea that bares her bosom to the moon;
The Winds that will be howling at all hours
And are up-gathered now like sleeping flowers;
For this, for every thing, we are out of tune;
It moves us not—Great God! I'd rather be
A Pagan suckled in a creed outworn;
So might I, standing on this pleasant lea,
Have glimpses that would make me less forlorn;
Have sight of Proteus coming from the sea;
Or hear old Triton blow his wreathed horn.

It is a beauteous Evening, calm and free;
The holy time is quiet as a Nun
Breathless with adoration; the broad sun
Is sinking down in its tranquillity;
The gentleness of heaven is on the Sea:
Listen! the mighty Being is awake
And doth with his eternal motion make
A sound like thunder—everlastingly.
Dear Child! dear Girl! that walkest with me here,
If thou appear'st untouched by solemn thought,
Thy nature is not therefore less divine:
Thou liest in Abraham's bosom all the year;
And worshipp'st at the Temple's inner shrine,
God being with thee when we know it not.

I grieved for Buonaparte, with a vain
And an unthinking grief! the vital blood
Of that Man's mind what can it be? What food
Fed his first hopes? What knowledge could He gain?
'Tis not in battles that from youth we train
The Governor who must be wise and good,
And temper with the sternness of the brain
Thoughts motherly, and meek as womanhood.
Wisdom doth live with children round her knees:
Books, leisure, perfect freedom, and the talk
Man holds with week-day man in the hourly walk
Of the mind's business: these are the degrees
By which true Sway doth mount; this is the stalk
True Power doth grow on; and her rights are these.

TO TOUSSAINT L'OUVERTURE

Toussaint, the most unhappy Man of Men!
Whether the rural Milk-maid by her Cow
Sing in thy hearing, or thou liest now
Alone in some deep dungeon's earless den,
O miserable chieftain! where and when
Wilt thou find patience? Yet die not; do thou
Wear rather in thy bonds a chearful brow:
Though fallen Thyself, never to rise again,
Live, and take comfort. Thou hast left behind
Powers that will work for thee; air, earth, and skies;
There's not a breathing of the common wind
That will forget thee; thou hast great allies;
Thy friends are exultations, agonies,
And love, and Man's unconquerable mind.

LONDON, 1802

Milton! thou should'st be living at this hour:
England hath need of thee: she is a fen
Of stagnant waters: altar, sword and pen,
Fireside, the heroic wealth of hall and bower,
Have forfeited their ancient English dower
Of inward happiness. We are selfish men;
Oh! raise us up, return to us again;
And give us manners, virtue, freedom, power.
Thy soul was like a Star and dwelt apart:
Thou hadst a voice whose sound was like the sea;
Pure as the naked heavens, majestic, free,
So didst thou travel on life's common way,
In chearful godliness; and yet thy heart
The lowliest duties on itself did lay.

Great Men have been among us; hands that penned
And tongues that uttered wisdom, better none:
The later Sydney, Marvel, Harrington,
Young Vane, and others who called Milton Friend.
These Moralists could act and comprehend:
They knew how genuine glory was put on;
Taught us how rightfully a nation shone
In splendor: what strength was, that would not bend
But in magnanimous meekness. France, 'tis strange,
Hath brought forth no such souls as we had then.
Perpetual emptiness! unceasing change!
No single Volume paramount, no code,
No master spirit, no determined road;
But equally a want of Books and Men!

It is not to be thought of that the Flood
Of British freedom, which to the open Sea
Of the world's praise from dark antiquity
Hath flowed, 'with pomp of waters, unwithstood,'
Road by which all might come and go that would,
And bear out freights of worth to foreign lands;
That this most famous Stream in Bogs and Sands
Should perish; and to evil and to good
Be lost for ever. In our Halls is hung
Armoury of the invincible Knights of old:
We must be free or die, who speak the tongue
That Shakespeare spake; the faith and morals hold
Which Milton held. In every thing we are sprung
Of Earth's first blood, have titles manifold.

THE SOLITARY REAPER

Behold her, single in the field,
Yon solitary Highland Lass!
Reaping and singing by herself;
Stop here, or gently pass!
Alone she cuts, and binds the grain,
And sings a melancholy strain;
O listen! for the Vale profound
Is overflowing with the sound.

No Nightingale did ever chaunt
So sweetly to reposing bands
Of Travellers in some shady haunt,
Among Arabian Sands:
No sweeter voice was ever heard
In spring-time from the Cuckoo-bird,
Breaking the silence of the seas
Among the farthest Hebrides.

Will no one tell me what she sings?
Perhaps the plaintive numbers flow
For old, unhappy, far-off things,
And battles long ago:
Or is it some more humble lay,
Familiar matter of today?
Some natural sorrow, loss, or pain,
That has been, and may be again!

Whate'er the theme, the Maiden sung
As if her song could have no ending;
I saw her singing at her work,
And o'er the sickle bending;
I listened till I had my fill;
And, as I mounted up the hill,
The music in my heart I bore,
Long after it was heard no more.

STEPPING WESTWARD

While my Fellow-traveller and I were walking by the side of
Loch Ketterine, one fine evening after sun-set, in our road to a
Hut where in the course of our Tour we had been hospitably
entertained some weeks before, we met, in one of the loneliest
parts of that solitary region, two well dressed Women, one of
whom said to us, by way of greeting, 'What you are stepping
Westward?'

'What you are stepping westward?'—'Yea'
—'Twould be a wildish destiny,
If we, who thus together roam
In a strange Land, and far from home,
Were in this place the guests of Chance:
Yet who would stop, or fear to advance,
Though home or shelter he had none,
With such a Sky to lead him on?

The dewy ground was dark and cold;
Behind, all gloomy to behold;
And stepping westward seemed to be
A kind of *heavenly* destiny;
I liked the greeting; 'twas a sound
Of something without place or bound;
And seemed to give me spiritual right
To travel through that region bright.

The voice was soft, and she who spake
Was walking by her native Lake:
The salutation had to me
The very sound of courtesy:
Its power was felt; and while my eye
Was fixed upon the glowing sky,

The echo of the voice enwrought
A human sweetness with the thought
Of travelling through the world that lay
Before me in my endless way.

YARROW UNVISITED

(See the various Poems the scene of which is laid upon the
Banks of the Yarrow; in particular, the exquisite Ballad of
Hamilton, beginning
    'Busk ye, busk ye my bonny, bonny Bride,
    Busk ye, busk ye my winsome Marrow!'—)

From Stirling Castle we had seen
The mazy Forth unravelled;
Had trod the banks of Clyde, and Tay,
And with the Tweed had travelled;
And, when we came to Clovenford,
Then said my *'winsome Marrow'*,
'Whate'er betide, we'll turn aside,
And see the Braes of Yarrow.'

'Let Yarrow Folk, *frae* Selkirk Town,
Who have been buying, selling,
Go back to Yarrow, 'tis their own,
Each Maiden to her Dwelling!
On Yarrow's Banks let herons feed,
Hares couch, and rabbits burrow!
But we will downwards with the Tweed,
Nor turn aside to Yarrow.'

'There's Galla Water, Leader Haughs,
Both lying right before us;
And Dryborough, where with chiming Tweed
The Lintwhites sing in chorus;
There's pleasant Tiviot Dale, a land
Made blithe with plough and harrow;
Why throw away a needful day
To go in search of Yarrow?'

'What's Yarrow but a River bare
That glides the dark hills under?
There are a thousand such elsewhere
As worthy of your wonder.'
—Strange words they seemed of slight and scorn;
My True-love sighed for sorrow;
And looked me in the face, to think
I thus could speak of Yarrow!

'Oh! green,' said I, 'are Yarrow's Holms,
And sweet is Yarrow flowing!
Fair hangs the apple frae the rock,*
But we will leave it growing.
O'er hilly path, and open Strath,
We'll wander Scotland thorough;
But, though so near, we will not turn
Into the Dale of Yarrow.'

'Let Beeves and home-bred Kine partake
The sweets of Burn-mill meadow;
The Swan on still St. Mary's Lake
Float double, Swan and Shadow!
We will not see them; will not go,
Today, nor yet tomorrow;
Enough if in our hearts we know,
There's such a place as Yarrow.'

* See Hamilton's Ballad as above.

'Be Yarrow Stream unseen, unknown!
It must, or we shall rue it:
We have a vision of our own;
Ah! why should we undo it?
The treasured dreams of times long past
We'll keep them, winsome Marrow!
For when we're there although 'tis fair
'Twill be another Yarrow!'

'If Care with freezing years should come,
And wandering seem but folly,
Should we be loth to stir from home,
And yet be melancholy;
Should life be dull, and spirits low,
'Twill soothe us in our sorrow
That earth has something yet to show,
The bonny Holms of Yarrow!'

TO A BUTTERFLY

Stay near me—do not take thy flight!
A little longer stay in sight!
Much converse do I find in Thee,
Historian of my Infancy!
Float near me; do not yet depart!
Dead times revive in thee:
Thou bring'st, gay Creature as thou art!
A solemn image to my heart,
My Father's Family!

Oh! pleasant, pleasant were the days,
The time, when in our childish plays
My Sister Emmeline and I
Together chaced the Butterfly!
A very hunter did I rush
Upon the prey:—with leaps and springs
I followed on from brake to bush;
But She, God love her! feared to brush
The dust from off its wings.

My heart leaps up when I behold
    A Rainbow in the sky:
So was it when my life began;
So is it now I am a Man;
So be it when I shall grow old,
    Or let me die!
The Child is Father of the Man;
And I could wish my days to be
Bound each to each by natural piety.

WRITTEN IN MARCH,

*while resting on the Bridge at
the Foot of Brother's Water.*

The cock is crowing,
The stream is flowing,
The small birds twitter,
The lake doth glitter,
The green field sleeps in the sun;
The oldest and youngest
Are at work with the strongest;
The cattle are grazing,
Their heads never raising;
There are forty feeding like one!
Like an army defeated
The Snow hath retreated,
And now doth fare ill
On the top of the bare hill;
The Plough-boy is whooping—anon—anon:
There's joy in the mountains;
There's life in the fountains;
Small clouds are sailing,
Blue sky prevailing;
The rain is over and gone!

THE SMALL CELANDINE

There is a Flower, the Lesser Celandine,
That shrinks, like many more, from cold and rain;
And, the first moment that the sun may shine,
Bright as the sun itself, 'tis out again!

When hailstones have been falling swarm on swarm,
Or blasts the green field and the trees distressed,
Oft have I seen it muffled up from harm,
In close self-shelter, like a Thing at rest.

But lately, one rough day, this Flower I passed,
And recognized it, though an altered Form,
Now standing forth an offering to the Blast,
And buffetted at will by Rain and Storm.

I stopped, and said with inly muttered voice,
'It doth not love the shower, nor seek the cold:
This neither is it's courage nor it's choice,
But it's necessity in being old.

The sunshine may not bless it, nor the dew;
It cannot help itself in it's decay;
Stiff in it's members, withered, changed of hue.'
And, in my spleen, I smiled that it was grey.

To be a Prodigal's Favorite—then, worse truth,
A Miser's Pensioner—behold our lot!
O Man! that from thy fair and shining youth
Age might but take the things Youth needed not!

I wandered lonely as a Cloud
That floats on high o'er Vales and Hills,
When all at once I saw a crowd
A host of dancing Daffodils;
Along the Lake, beneath the trees,
Ten thousand dancing in the breeze.

The waves beside them danced, but they
Outdid the sparkling waves in glee:—
A Poet could not but be gay
In such a laughing company:
I gazed—and gazed—but little thought
What wealth the shew to me had brought:

For oft when on my couch I lie
In vacant or in pensive mood,
They flash upon that inward eye
Which is the bliss of solitude,
And then my heart with pleasure fills,
And dances with the Daffodils.

TO THE CUCKOO

O blithe New-comer! I have heard,
I hear thee and rejoice:
O Cuckoo! shall I call thee Bird,
Or but a wandering Voice?

While I am lying on the grass,
I hear thy restless shout:
From hill to hill it seems to pass,
About, and all about!

To me, no Babbler with a tale
Of sunshine and of flowers,
Thou tellest, Cuckoo! in the vale
Of visionary hours.

Thrice welcome, Darling of the Spring!
Even yet thou art to me
No Bird; but an invisible Thing,
A voice, a mystery.

The same whom in my School-boy days
I listened to; that Cry
Which made me look a thousand ways;
In bush, and tree, and sky.

To seek thee did I often rove
Through woods and on the green;
And thou wert still a hope, a love;
Still longed for, never seen!

And I can listen to thee yet;
Can lie upon the plain.
And listen, till I do beget
That golden time again.

O blessed Bird! the earth we pace
Again appears to be
An unsubstantial, faery place;
That is fit home for Thee!

TO A BUTTERFLY

I've watched you now a full half hour,
Self-poised upon that yellow flower;
And, little Butterfly! indeed
I know not if you sleep, or feed.
How motionless! not frozen seas
More motionless! and then
What joy awaits you, when the breeze
Hath found you out among the trees,
And calls you forth again!

This plot of Orchard-ground is ours;
My trees they are, my Sister's flowers;
Stop here whenever you are weary,
And rest as in a sanctuary!
Come often to us, fear no wrong;
Sit near us on the bough!
We'll talk of sunshine and of song;
And summer days, when we were young,
Sweet childish days, that were as long
   As twenty days are now!

A COMPLAINT

There is a change—and I am poor;
Your Love hath been, nor long ago,
A Fountain at my fond Heart's door,
Whose only business was to flow;
And flow it did; not taking heed
Of its own bounty, or my need.

What happy moments did I count!
Blessed was I then all bliss above!
Now, for this consecrated Fount
Of murmuring, sparkling, living love,
What have I? shall I dare to tell?
A comfortless, and hidden WELL.

A Well of love—it may be deep—
I trust it is, and never dry:
What matter? if the Waters sleep
In silence and obscurity.
—Such change, and at the very door
Of my fond Heart, hath made me poor.

ELEGIAC STANZAS,

*suggested by a Picture of Peele Castle, in
a Storm, painted by Sir George Beaumont.*

I was thy Neighbour once, thou rugged Pile!
Four summer weeks I dwelt in sight of thee:
I saw thee every day; and all the while
Thy Form was sleeping on a glassy sea.

So pure the sky, so quiet was the air!
So like, so very like, was day to day!
When'er I looked, thy Image still was there;
It trembled, but it never passed away.

How perfect was the calm! it seemed no sleep;
No mood, which season takes away, or brings:
I could have fancied that the mighty Deep
Was even the gentlest of all gentle Things.

Ah! THEN, if mine had been the Painter's hand,
To express what then I saw; and add the gleam,
The light that never was, on sea or land,
The consecration, and the Poet's dream;

I would have planted thee, thou hoary Pile!
Amid a world how different from this!
Beside a sea that could not cease to smile;
On tranquil land, beneath a sky of bliss:

Thou shouldst have seemed a treasure-house, a mine
Of peaceful years; a chronicle of heaven:—
Of all the sunbeams that did ever shine
The very sweetest had to thee been given.

A Picture had it been of lasting ease,
Elysian quiet, without toil or strife;
No motion but the moving tide, a breeze,
Or merely silent Nature's breathing life.

Such, in the fond delusion of my heart,
Such Picture would I at that time have made:
And seen the soul of truth in every part;
A faith, a trust, that could not be betrayed.

So once it would have been,—'tis so no more;
I have submitted to a new controul:
A power is gone, which nothing can restore;
A deep distress hath humanized my Soul.

Not for a moment could I now behold
A smiling sea and be what I have been:
The feeling of my loss will ne'er be old;
This, which I know, I speak with mind serene.

Then, Beaumont, Friend! who would have been the Friend,
If he had lived, of Him whom I deplore,
This Work of thine I blame not, but commend;
This sea in anger, and that dismal shore.

Oh 'tis a passionate Work!—yet wise and well;
Well chosen is the spirit that is here;
That Hulk which labours in the deadly swell,
This rueful sky, this pageantry of fear!

And this huge Castle, standing here sublime,
I love to see the look with which it braves,
Cased in the unfeeling armour of old time,
The light'ning, the fierce wind, and trampling waves.

Farewell, farewell the Heart that lives alone,
Housed in a dream, at distance from the Kind!
Such happiness, wherever it be known,
Is to be pitied; for 'tis surely blind.

But welcome fortitude, and patient chear,
And frequent sights of what is to be born!
Such sights, or worse, as are before me here.—
Not without hope we suffer and we mourn.

ODE

Paolò majora canamus

ODE

There was a time when meadow, grove, and stream,
The earth, and every common sight,
        To me did seem
        Apparelled in celestial light,
The glory and the freshness of a dream.
It is not now as it has been of yore;—
        Turn wheresoe'er I may,
            By night or day,
The things which I have seen I now can see no more.

        The Rainbow comes and goes,
        And lovely is the Rose,
        The Moon doth with delight
        Look round her when the heavens are bare;
            Waters on a starry night
            Are beautiful and fair;
        The sunshine is a glorious birth;
        But yet I know, where'er I go,
That there hath passed away a glory from the earth.

Now, while the Birds thus sing a joyous song,
        And while the young Lambs bound
            As to the tabor's sound,
To me alone there came a thought of grief:
A timely utterance gave that thought relief,
            And I again am strong.
The Cataracts blow their trumpets from the steep,
No more shall grief of mine the season wrong;
I hear the Echoes through the mountains throng,
The Winds come to me from the fields of sleep,

And all the earth is gay,
    Land and sea
Give themselves up to jollity,
    And with the heart of May
Doth every Beast keep holiday,
    Thou Child of Joy
Shout round me, let me hear thy shouts, thou happy
                    Shepherd Boy!

Ye blessed Creatures, I have heard the call
    Ye to each other make; I see
The heavens laugh with you in your jubilee;
    My heart is at your festival,
    My head hath its coronal,
The fullness of your bliss, I feel—I feel it all.
    Oh evil day! if I were sullen
    While the Earth herself is adorning,
        This sweet May-morning,
    And the Children are pulling,
        On every side,
    In a thousand vallies far and wide,
    Fresh flowers; while the sun shines warm,
And the Babe leaps up on his mother's arm:—
    I hear, I hear, with joy I hear!
    —But there's a Tree, of many one,
A single Field which I have looked upon,
Both of them speak of something that is gone:
        The Pansy at my feet
        Doth the same tale repeat:
Whither is fled the visionary gleam?
Where is it now, the glory and the dream?

Our birth is but a sleep and a forgetting:
The Soul that rises with us, our life's Star,
        Hath had elsewhere its setting,
            And cometh from afar:
        Not in entire forgetfulness,
        And not in utter nakedness,
But trailing clouds of glory do we come
        From God, who is our home:
Heaven lies about us in our infancy!
Shades of the prison-house begin to close
        Upon the growing Boy,
But He beholds the light, and whence it flows,
        He sees it in his joy;
The Youth, who daily farther from the East
        Must travel, still is Nature's Priest,
            And by the vision splendid
            Is on his way attended;
At length the Man perceives it die away,
And fade into the light of common day.

Earth fills her lap with pleasures of her own;
Yearnings she hath in her own natural kind,
And, even with something of a Mother's mind,
        And no unworthy aim,
    The homely Nurse doth all she can
To make her Foster-child, her Inmate Man,
        Forget the glories he hath known,
And that imperial palace whence he came.

Behold the Child among his new-born blisses,
A four year's Darling of a pigmy size!
See, where 'mid work of his own hand he lies,
Fretted by sallies of his Mother's kisses,
With light upon him from his Father's eyes!
See, at his feet, some little plan or chart,
Some fragment from his dream of human life,
Shaped by himself with newly-learned art;
  A wedding or a festival,
  A mourning or a funeral;
   And this hath now his heart,
  And unto this he frames his song:
   Then will he fit his tongue
To dialogues of business, love, or strife;
  But it will not be long
  Ere this be thrown aside,
  And with new joy and pride
The little Actor cons another part,
Filling from time to time his 'humorous stage'
With all the Persons, down to palsied Age,
That Life brings with her in her Equipage;
  As if his whole vocation
  Were endless imitation.

Thou, whose exterior semblance doth belie
  Thy Soul's immensity;
Thou best Philosopher, who yet dost keep
Thy heritage, thou Eye among the blind,
That, deaf and silent, read'st the eternal deep,
Haunted for ever by the eternal mind,—
  Mighty Prophet! Seer blest!
  On whom those truths do rest,

Which we are toiling all our lives to find;
Thou, over whom thy Immortality
Broods like the Day, a Master o'er a Slave,
A Presence which is not to be put by;
      To whom the grave
Is but a lonely bed without the sense or sight
      Of day or the warm light,
A place of thought where we in waiting lie;
Thou little Child, yet glorious in the might
Of untamed pleasures, on thy Being's height,
Why with such earnest pains dost thou provoke
The Years to bring the inevitable yoke,
Thus blindly with thy blessedness at strife?
Full soon thy Soul shall have her earthly freight,
And custom lie upon thee with a weight,
Heavy as frost, and deep almost as life!

      O joy! that in our embers
      Is something that doth live,
      That nature yet remembers
      What was so fugitive!
The thought of our past years in me doth breed
Perpetual benedictions: not indeed
For that which is most worthy to be blest;
Delight and liberty, the simple creed
Of Childhood, whether fluttering or at rest,
With new-born hope for ever in his breast:—
      Not for these I raise
      The song of thanks and praise;
      But for those obstinate questionings
      Of sense and outward things,
      Fallings from us, vanishings;

Blank misgivings of a Creature
Moving about in worlds not realized,
High instincts, before which our mortal Nature
Did tremble like a guilty Thing surprized:
But for those first affections,
Those shadowy recollections,
Which, be they what they may,
Are yet the fountain light of all our day,
Are yet a master light of all our seeing;
Uphold us, cherish us, and make
Our noisy years seem moments in the being
Of the eternal Silence: truths that wake,
To perish never;
Which neither listlessness, nor mad endeavour,
Nor Man nor Boy,
Nor all that is at enmity with joy,
Can utterly abolish or destroy!
Hence, in a season of calm weather,
Though inland far we be,
Our Souls have sight of that immortal sea
Which brought us hither,
Can in a moment travel thither,
And see the Children sport upon the shore,
And hear the mighty waters rolling evermore.

Then, sing ye Birds, sing, sing a joyous song!
And let the young Lambs bound
As to the tabor's sound!
We in thought will join your throng,
Ye that pipe and ye that play,
Ye that through your hearts today
Feel the gladness of the May!

What though the radiance which was once so bright
Be now for ever taken from my sight,
        Though nothing can bring back the hour
Of splendour in the grass, of glory in the flower;
            We will grieve not, rather find
            Strength in what remains behind,
            In the primal sympathy
            Which having been must ever be,
            In the soothing thoughts that spring
            Out of human suffering,
            In the faith that looks through death,
In years that bring the philosophic mind.

And oh ye Fountains, Meadows, Hills, and Groves,
Think not of any severing of our loves!
Yet in my heart of hearts I feel your might;
I only have relinquished one delight
To live beneath your more habitual sway.
I love the Brooks which down their channels fret,
Even more than when I tripped lightly as they;
The innocent brightness of a new-born Day
            Is lovely yet;
The Clouds that gather round the setting sun
Do take a sober colouring from an eye
That hath kept watch o'er man's mortality;
Another race hath been, and other palms are won.
Thanks to the human heart by which we live,
Thanks to its tenderness, its joys, and fears,
To me the meanest flower that blows can give
Thoughts that do often lie too deep for tears.

LATER POEMS

Surprized by joy—impatient as the Wind
I wished to share the transport—Oh! with whom
But Thee, long buried in the silent Tomb,
That spot which no vicissitude can find?
Love, faithful love recalled thee to my mind—
But how could I forget thee!—Through what power,
Even for the least division of an hour,
Have I been so beguiled as to be blind
To my most grievous loss?—That thought's return
Was the worst pang that sorrow ever bore,
Save one, one only, when I stood forlorn,
Knowing my heart's best treasure was no more;
That neither present time, nor years unborn
Could to my sight that heavenly face restore.

I wandered lonely as a Cloud
That floats on high o'er Vales and Hills,
When all at once I saw a crowd,
A host of golden Daffodils;
Beside the Lake, beneath the trees,
Fluttering and dancing in the breeze.

Continuous as the stars that shine
And twinkle on the milky way,
They stretched in never-ending line
Along the margin of a bay:
Ten thousand saw I at a glance,
Tossing their heads in sprightly dance.

The waves beside them danced, but they
Out-did the sparkling waves in glee:—
A Poet could not but be gay
In such a jocund company:
I gazed—and gazed—but little thought
What wealth the shew to me had brought:

For oft when on my couch I lie
In vacant or in pensive mood,
They flash upon that inward eye
Which is the bliss of solitude,
And then my heart with pleasure fills,
And dances with the Daffodils.

CONCLUSION to *THE RIVER DUDDON*

I thought of Thee, my partner and my guide,
As being passed away.—Vain sympathies!
For, *backward*, Duddon! as I cast my eyes,
I see what was, and is, and will abide;
Still glides the Stream, and shall for ever glide;
The Form remains, the Function never dies;
While *we*, the brave, the mighty, and the wise,
We Men, who in our morn of youth defied
The elements, must vanish;—be it so!
Enough, if something from our hands have power
To live, and act, and serve the future hour;
And if, as tow'rd the silent tomb we go,
Thro' love, thro' hope, and faith's transcendent dower,
We feel that we are greater than we know.

MUTABILITY

From low to high doth dissolution climb,
And sinks from high to low, along a scale
Of awful notes, whose concord shall not fail;
A musical but melancholy chime,
Which they can hear who meddle not with crime,
Nor avarice, nor over-anxious care.
Truth fails not; but her outward forms that bear
The longest date do melt like frosty rime,
That in the morning whitened hill and plain
And is no more; drop like the tower sublime
Of yesterday, which royally did wear
Its crown of weeds, but could not even sustain
Some casual shout that broke the silent air,
Or the unimaginable touch of Time.

AIREY-FORCE VALLEY

——Not a breath of air
Ruffles the bosom of this leafy glen.
From the brook's margin, wide around, the trees
Are stedfast as the rocks; the brook itself,
Old as the hills that feed it from afar,
Doth rather deepen than disturb the calm
Where all things else are still and motionless.
And yet, even now, a little breeze, perchance
Escaped from boisterous winds that rage without,
Has entered, by the sturdy oaks unfelt,
But to its gentle touch how sensitive
Is the light ash! that, pendent from the brow
Of yon dim cave, in seeming silence makes
A soft eye-music of slow-waving boughs,
Powerful almost as vocal harmony
To stay the wanderer's steps and soothe his thoughts.

EXTEMPORE EFFUSION
Upon the Death of James Hogg

When first, descending from the moorlands,
I saw the Stream of Yarrow glide
Along a bare and open valley,
The Ettrick Shepherd was my guide.

When last along its banks I wandered,
Through groves that had begun to shed
Their golden leaves upon the pathways,
My steps the border minstrel led.

The mighty Minstrel breathes no longer,
'Mid mouldering ruins low he lies;
And death upon the braes of Yarrow,
Has closed the Shepherd-poet's eyes:

Nor has the rolling year twice measured,
From sign to sign, its stedfast course,
Since every mortal power of Coleridge
Was frozen at its marvellous source;

The 'rapt One, of the godlike forehead,
The heaven-eyed creature sleeps in earth:
And Lamb, the frolic and the gentle,
Has vanished from his lonely hearth.

Like clouds that rake the mountain-summits,
Or waves that own no curbing hand,
How fast has brother followed brother,
From sunshine to the sunless land!

[272]

Yet I, whose lids from infant slumbers
Were earlier raised, remain to hear
A timid voice, that asks in whispers,
'Who next will drop and disappear?'

Our haughty life is crowned with darkness,
Like London with its own black wreath,
On which with thee, O Crabbe! forth-looking,
I gazed from Hampstead's breezy heath.

As if but yesterday departed,
Thou too art gone before; but why,
O'er ripe fruit, seasonably gathered,
Should frail survivors heave a sigh?

Mourn rather for that holy Spirit,
Sweet as the spring, as ocean deep;
For Her who, ere her summer faded,
Has sunk into a breathless sleep.

No more of old romantic sorrows,
For slaughtered Youth or love-lorn Maid!
With sharper grief is Yarrow smitten,
And Ettrick mourns with her their Poet dead.

TITLES AND FIRST LINES